COMMUNITY ACTION SOURCEBOOK

Toward Empowerment of People

Theodore Lownik Library
Illinois Benedictine College
Lisle, Illinois 60532

by
Sheila Macmanus

*To the Theodore Lownik Library
of Illinois Benedictine College*

Sheila Macmanus

**Paulist Press
New York/Ramsey**

Copyright © 1983 by
Sheila Macmanus

All rights reserved.

Library of Congress
Catalog Card Number:
82-60854

ISBN:
0-8091-2472-6

Published by Paulist Press
545 Island Road
Ramsey, N.J. 07446

Printed and bound in the
United States of America

To my Mom and Dad, Rita and Armand Macmanus

Contents

    Introduction 9

I. Theoretical Orientations/
    Ethical Considerations 15

II. Community Action Profiles 19

    National Networks/Organizations   19
    Individual Projects/Groups: A Sampler   33

III. Factsheets 49

    The Aged   49
    Child Development and Youth   53
    Criminal Justice   58
    Drugs and Addiction   63
    Economic Development   67
    Education   71
    The Environment   73
    The Handicapped   79
    Housing   83
    Hunger   87
    Legal Aid   90
    Minorities   92
    Welfare   96
    Women   99

IV. Supplementary Address List 101
    Notes 105

"He who cannot change the very fabric of his thought will never be able to change reality and will never, therefore, make any progress."
—**Anwar Sadat**

"Those who hope to change things massively often miss the first meaning of human change, which is to submit oneself to change...."
—**Daniel Berrigan**

Acknowledgments

Thanks for advice, information, and interest to Harry Fagan in Cleveland, Marv Mottet in Washington, D.C., Chuck Orlebeke, Rob Mier, and Bob Stark in Chicago.

The ACORN staff in New Orleans, Thomas Johns of Community Training and Development in Fond du Lac, Wisconsin, George Spellman and staff of Joint Action in Community Service in Washington, D.C., the staff of the National Association of Neighborhoods in Washington, D.C., Lawrence Wilson at the National Center for Community Action in Washington, D.C., and Elton Jolly of the Opportunities Industrialization Centers of America in Philadelphia—all supplied useful information.

Thank you to the community action staffs of projects across the country who took the time to respond to my questionnaire. All the information received contributed to the perspectives in this book. Special thanks go to Sr. Jean Abbott and Gina Ryan of the St. Louis Association of Community Organizations; Shelly Benkaim of the Iowa ACORN in Davenport (and Des Moines); Tobia Cuney of the West Oakland Food Project in Oakland, California; Catherine Dufault, R.S.M., of the Citizens League of Woonsocket (Rhode Island) Together; the Farmworkers Legal Services of New York in Rochester; Eileen

Haggerty of the Michigan Coalition on Utilities and Energy in Detroit; Marc Hand of the Voces Unidas Bilingual Broadcasting Foundation in Salinas, California; Warren Hanson of the West Bank Community Development Corporation in Minneapolis; Mark Kleiman of the Consumer Coalition for Health in Washington, D.C.; Mark Peterson of the Pennsylvania Alliance on Jobs and Energy in Pittsburgh; John Reilly of the Fordham Bedford Housing Corporation in the Bronx in New York City; and Bebe Verdery of the Jenkinsville Energy/Health Project in Jenkinsville, South Carolina.

Thanks to Matthew, Nathaniel, and Adam Fahey, Ray Heise, and Pat Ivarra for interest in and support of my work on this sourcebook.

Introduction

This is a book about community action. It is written for persons acting in groups or in networks of groups with the purpose of solving social problems and meeting social challenges in their communities and localities.

It is a book of tools which is divided into four sections. Section I, Theoretical Orientations/Ethical Considerations, is a short piece intended to stimulate reflection about ethical orientations to (the means and ends of) community action.

Section II, Community Action Profiles, is divided into two subparts. The first part profiles three prominent national organizations which are involved in community action: the Association of Community Organizations for Reform Now (ACORN), the National Association of Neighborhoods (N.A.N.), and the Opportunities Industrialization Centers of America (OIC/A). Each is described according to the following outline: history, philosophy and goals, structure, funding, organizing methodologies, and examples of activities.

The second subpart of Section II is a sampler of ten smaller local groups/projects/organizations. These profiles are of three multi-issue local community action organizations (one of which is affiliated with ACORN), one diocesan social action commission, two neighborhood commercial ventures (drugstore, food co-op), one neighborhood housing development corporation, one consumer health coalition, one area communications venture (bilingual radio station), and one local group with a focus on energy and the utilities. Each group is described, structure delineated, sources of funding pinpointed, and community action methodologies (successful and unsuccessful) listed. The connection of each project to religious institutions is pointed out.

This subpart is the result of my query of a variety of forty groups or projects which were evenly distributed nationwide.

All of the organizations and projects profiled in Section II are non-governmental, although several enter into contracts with government entities to provide services locally. The ten smaller organizations/projects are all connected to religious institutions. The connection may be direct (as that of the diocesan social action commission) or less direct (as those partially funded by a church-related agent such as the Campaign for Human Development, Catholic Charities, or a religious community).

It should be noted that throughout this section you will find reference to the Campaign for Human Development of the U.S. Catholic Conference. The CHD is a key funding source for a multitude of projects nationwide. When referred to as a funding source in this section, it means that CHD has been a funding source for at least one year of the program or project in question.

It should also be (foot)noted that I put information provided me by the national organizations and local groups into uniform formats, using their words as much as possible. Each organization in question was aware of the possible use of the information supplied as part of this book, and all were most encouraging.

All of the organizations mentioned in Section II see that the central strength of a community organization is its community support—the broader-based, the better. In their questionnaire responses the local projects agreed across the board with the Community Training and Development Organization's definition of community action: "people helping people help themselves." They all touted a democratic structure as a key to effectiveness.

Section III lists facts, thoughts to ponder, and resources available with respect to fourteen areas of challenge to community groups: the Aged, Child Development and Youth, Criminal Justice, Drugs and Addiction, Economic Development, Education, the Environment, the Handicapped, Housing, Hunger, Legal Aid, Minorities, Welfare, and Women.

The treatment is of varying lengths, with more basic issues (environment, criminal justice, child development and youth) receiving greater attention than do others. (If we poison the environment and make life on the planet impossible, the question of whether old people have a difficult time living on fixed incomes becomes moot.)

Section IV is a Supplementary Address List. (Key addresses for given issue areas are found in the factsheet section for each issue.) These additional addresses of interest are listed alphabetically. Space is left at the end of this section for you to add your own frequently used community action addresses.

Throughout the book if there was a choice in any given instance, I kept the focus on the national level so that the information would be useful across the board. Contacting the national organizations mentioned will lead you to the local groups and resources which may be of more use to you and your group.

Occasionally I have mentioned only government policy and its effects in a given area. Much of the activity (or constraints on activity) in the area of economic development, for example, has been from the public sector. I leave it to the community group to review what government at all levels is doing in a given area of concern. Many of the most effective community action efforts use public/private sector collaboration to achieve solid gains.

Larger issues such as the effects of our national defense posture, our human rights posture, macro- and micro-economics, inflation, etc., on life and possibilities for community are not touched on in this book except very indirectly. Quality of life areas such as the arts, media, and recreation and resource development in these areas are ignored, although positive action in these areas could be preventive medicine for the social problems discussed. None of the above should be overlooked by groups as possible areas for worthwhile community action.

A word about government

Initially I had intended to include a factsheet on government. The topic proved too unwieldy to condense into readily useful form. Some discussion is warranted, however.

At the Federal level as of 1980 there were, in addition to the President, the White House staff, and the executive agencies (Council of Economic Advisors, CIA, OMB, etc.), sixteen Departments and sixty-two independent agencies (Consumer Product Safety Commission, Library of Congress, Securities and Exchange Commission, Veterans Administration, etc.).

Often much emphasis in our society is placed on government at the Federal level because Federal activities affect everyone. For the local community action organization, however, state level politics may be of far more crucial import than Federal level politics. In lieu of a factsheet focusing on state level government alone, I excerpt Toby Moffett's excellent book, *Nobody's Business: The Political Intruder's Guide to Everyone's State Legislature:*

The fifty state legislatures hold powers which directly and personally influence our lives, and yet the fact that no one sees them as grist for the literary mills is hardly surprising. True, the states tell us when we can marry, on what grounds we may divorce, whether our sexual practices are legal, how qualified our medical doctors must be, whether we are eligible for welfare, what taxes we must pay and how they are to be spent. In addition, the states establish criminal codes under which we may be arrested, maintain the courts in which we are tried and supervise the prisons where we may languish or become rehabilitated. In the end, the states tell us how we may dispose of our estates and how much our heirs may keep.

But who cares? How exciting can a legislature be that meets part-time (as most do), has little if any staff, offers few individual offices in which to keep files, pays its members next to nothing (thus ensuring the domination of those who can financially afford to be there—lawyers and other self-employed professionals), has too many committees with far too many members for efficiency and works in the ever-present shadow of the governor?

The products and services that federal, state, and local governments offer individuals and communities should be judged as any unit of economic output: by measures of effectiveness and efficiency. Effectiveness is high if user satisfaction is up; efficiency is high if cost per unit is as low as possible. It is difficult to assess the effectiveness of government or any other social services, but it is relatively simple to measure efficiency. With respect to human services, this is problematic because there are services which *some* entity *must* provide the needy, even if these services are costly to deliver.

The Federal government is officially involved in community action per se via the Community Services Administration (formerly OEO). Other key community *development* efforts such as the Community Development Block Grants and Revenue Sharing emanate elsewhere. The CSA provides seed money and oversees the activities of Community Action Agencies (CAAs). CAAs are locally controlled independent entities. The poor have full participation in policy making in the nearly 900 CAAs nationwide. Although the CAAs administer local anti-poverty programs totaling approximately $2.5 billion nationwide, Community Services Administration funds for CAA operations total only approximately one-fifth of that amount. In addition, each agency must match its Federal allotment with a percentage of locally generated funds.

Local community groups should be made aware of the National Center for Community Action, established in 1974 by the National Community Action Agency Executive Directors Association. Initially funded with a Community Services Administration grant, NCCA

is a private nonprofit corporation with offices in Washington, D.C. It provides an ongoing and comprehensive program of research, information, training, technical and other supportive services to CAAs. It is guided by a Board of Directors composed of 28 members. Twenty represent community action agencies at all levels and from all 10 Federal regions. Other members serve for national organizations with low-income and minority interests . . . .

NCCA has three organizational components: *Research and Information* collects, analyzes, and distributes information on Federal administrative and legislative developments affecting the poor. Its focus is at the national level; it is concerned with specific programs that CAAs can tap for funds and other resources and with general Federal policy trends. Its services include *The Reporter*, a bimonthly journal of in-depth and timely articles on low-income issues; *Counteraction*, a biweekly publication with the latest in new programs, regulations and programmatic developments; *NCCA Special Reports*, covering issues of more immediate or special concern to CAAs; special research projects and monographs, such as Where the Money Is!, a digest of Federal funding sources for nonprofit organizations; and a Washington information service that handles mail, telephone and personal requests for program information on an individual case-by-case basis. *Field Services* designs and delivers training programs and provides technical assistance on issues that are of major concern to CAA staff and board members . . . . *Network Services* links NCCA with the local CAAs and related organizations. It serves as a clearinghouse for local CAA programs, collecting, recording and distributing information that is utilized by (many groups) . . . . The department's services include a Program Information Network, listing and describing hundreds of specific CAA programs. *Human Work for Human Needs* is an NCCA publication that highlights CAA activities nationwide.

In dealing with government at all levels, local community action groups will likely encounter an organizational chasm between departments of human (social) services and departments of planning.

If I could offer one challenge to the community groups using this book, it would be to imagine a society which engages not in "delivering" social services *and* planning to "clients," but a society which engages in the art of *social planning* by empowered people for humane communities.

Peace!

I. Theoretical Orientations/Ethical Considerations

Social action rests on a base which is at once religious and ethical. Religion includes ethics, for religion involves practicing values of the ideal life as well as seeking them out. To be ethical is to be high principled, to imbue one's life with right conduct and right practices.

For the Christian, the end of the ideal life is reached by the means of ethical practices. Although the means are various, the end of community action as described in this book is a meaningful life for all human beings. In order to live a meaningful life the world must be meaningfully constructed. The basic moral imperative, then, which validates social action efforts and forms them is the simple thesis that "human beings have the right to live in a meaningful world."[1]

Social problems, social disorder, get in the way of a meaningful world, meaningful communities, meaningful lives. Informed, reflective action—especially by groups—can do much to meaningfully reconstruct life on our planet. "Social construction, no less than music or landscape painting, represents the replacement by mind of a blind process for bringing order out of chaos."[2] Or to adapt Johannes B. Metz's definition of political theology, our methods will serve to counter man's privatizing tendency as we attempt to bring order, the eschatological message, out of chaos, the conditions of present society.[3]

Whom are we serving? The powerless, ourselves included.

How do we know what will make life more meaningful for people? Ask them. No aspect of social life "can be understood without looking into the question of what it means to those who participate in it."[4]

Many who are currently involved in community action and community development efforts lived through the perilous Community Action Program experience of the 1960s. We saw maximum feasible participation turn into, in Daniel Moynihan's words, "maximum feasible misunderstanding." Peter Berger and Richard Neuhaus in their book *To Empower People: The Role of Mediating Structures in Public Policy* tell us:

That experience (CAP) in no way invalidates the idea of community participation. First, the peculiar developments of the 1960s made that decade the worst possible time to try out the idea . . . . Second, and much more important, the institutions used to facilitate community participation were not the actual institutions of the community but were created by those in charge of the program. This was especially true in inner-city black areas—the chief focus of the program—where religious institutions were, for the most part, neglected or even deliberately undercut. So, to some extent, were the family structures of the black community. In short, the program's failures resulted precisely from its failure to utilize existing mediating structures.

This said, it remains true that mediating structures can be coopted by government, that they can become instruments of those interested in destroying rather than reforming American society, and that they can undermine the institutions of the formal polity. These are real risks. On the other side are the benefits . . . . Together they constitute a major challenge to the political imagination.[5]

So by working through existing community structures with a posture of listening to the powerless, it is possible to find out exactly what is needed and by whom.

With what *ethical* posture do we approach achieving our ends in society? Sociologist Max Weber spoke of two approaches, the ethics of attitude and the ethics of responsibility. The first requires that we adhere to absolute values regardless of the exigencies of the particular social situation. With the second attitude, involving an exercise of ethics of responsibility,

the political actor does not seek some inner purity in adherence to absolute norms, but, often, with anguished anxiety, tries to act in such a way as to effect the most humane consequence possible.[6]

In this second category Weber puts Machiavelli who esteemed the "welfare of his city higher than the salvation of his own soul."[7]

To the Christian, there must be some clean middle ground. We can achieve the possible in community action efforts, deal with the political powers that be, and still keep our hands unsoiled.

Although Weber's ethics of attitude sounds pure to the point of ineffectiveness, ethics of attitude does not by its nature nurture incapacity. If no one in the world could tighten even one bolt in the fuselage of a bomber without feeling morally impure, wars as we know them today would be non-existent, and perhaps we would have the calm to create a more humane world.

There is a good story which exemplifies ethics of responsibility and one which would have Machiavelli on his feet applauding. An activist friend likes to recount this episode in the political life of Louisiana's Huey Long (perhaps apocrypha or exaggeration but a mild and provocative example of what Weber was talking about):

A group in New Orleans fifty or so years ago wanted black women to be able to attend nursing school. Huey Long said he would guarantee they would get a brand new black nursing school but they had to agree not to call him down on his methods. The deal was sealed.

Soon after, Huey tours Charity Hospital with newsmen in tow and spies white nurses in black male wards. He explodes (best side to the newsreel cameras): "What are these white women doing touching these colored dudes! I won't stand for this. You're throwing these examples of fine southern young womanhood to these wolves! Let their own women do this work . . . ."

Huey did not have to ask the Louisiana legislature twice for the money to build a black nursing school.

My activist friend applauds Huey and his sense of the "possible" as well as his using racism to combat racism.

George McGovern recently offered a more extreme and easier-to-call example when he stated: "To abandon human rights in favor of combating terrorism is an operational impossibility because the suppression of human rights is itself an act of terrorism, sometimes of an exceedingly brutal nature . . . . (There is) the necessity of foreign policy goals and foreign policy methods that are themselves consistent with American democratic values."[8] McGovern is calling us to practice democracy impeccably. There is much to be said for Castaneda's Don Juan when he tells us that power is not in the hands of the warrior, but the warrior is in the hands of power. The warrior's "only freedom is to choose an impeccable life."[9]

The social scientist, the politician, and the "recipients" of policy had better get together to discuss the long range effects of the policy. We must look at the welfare of the city in more than the short term.

Of course there will be social costs with any social change, "disturbances in the order of meaning . . . the non-designed consequences that are possible."[10] We may be upsetting the order of meaning in the short term but in the longer term we are creating true order out of thinly disguised chaos.

In reflecting on the worthiness and worthwhileness of our means in social action it is a valuable exercise to draw a continuum. Place ethics of attitude at one end and ethics of responsibility at the other. Try to place Jesus of Nazareth on the line. Place yourself. Place your community organization. Place your policy decisions.

A society's social policies are connected to somebody's values. Weber tells us that commitment to ethical and cultural values is a *sine qua non* of worthwhile political activity.[11] Every action or policy idea or program should be able to withstand the basic question: Does it add to the meaning of people's lives?

It is still enormously difficult at times to find agreement on what would be meaningful, which goal should be pursued by what policy, what system should be adopted in implementing the policy.

In *Pyramids of Sacrifice*, Peter Berger offers a starting place:

> There is also . . . the difficult and politically motivated task of arriving at ethical propositions that might also be acceptable to those who cannot agree with one's own system. I think that such an enterprise will most profitably begin with negative starting points. That is, it will not begin by seeking assent to some common denominator between conflicting ethical systems (say, between Christians and Marxists, or between conservatives and liberals), but rather by looking at specific situations in which there will be a common "no" . . . *no* to children living in garbage, *no* to exploitation and hunger, *no* to terror and totalitarianism, *no* to anomie and the mindless destruction of human beings . . . . From these concrete instances of saying *no* one may then move ahead to the painstaking task of finding alternatives which will not only be morally acceptable, but which will work.[12]

In judging the ethics of our means and/against the essential worthiness of our ends, the words of St. Augustine are a touchstone: "I know nothing but this, that things fleeting and transitory should be spurned, that things certain and eternal should be sought."

II. Community Action Profiles

National Networks/Organizations

ACORN (Association of Community Organizations for Reform Now) Organizing and Support Center: 628 Baronne, New Orleans, Louisiana 70113, 504-523-1691
National Office: 1638 R Street, Washington, D.C. 20009

"A grass roots organization of low and moderate income people who have joined together to improve their communities and win a fairer share and greater voice for all low and moderate income Americans"

History
Drawing on the unique experience of the Southern Tenant Farmers Union in the 1930s, ACORN was established in 1970 as the Arkansas Community Organization for Reform Now

Philosophy/Goals

- overall thrust is gaining power for the disenfranchised, not just winning issues

- 6 key concepts form the philosophical base for ACORN
  —since the fundamental issue to be dealt with is the distribution of power in this country ACORN is more concerned with who

should have the power to determine how public funds are spent than on how the funds are spent

–power can only be achieved through organizing the "majority constituency" (the powerless); ACORN has traditionally defined the powerless as low to moderate income persons or the majority of persons in this country

–since limiting your issues means limiting your constituency and therefore your power, ACORN is a multi-issue organization

–unless the state is controlled by low and moderate income persons it will be difficult if not impossible to have any control over issues; involvement in electoral politics is the process with control of local government the goal (ACORN has endorsed non-ACORN member candidates and has run ACORN members for political office; ACORN groups have also addressed themselves to certain of the preconditions for effective political action, e.g., organizing change-of-government initiative campaigns designed to replace at-large systems of election with ward-by-ward or neighborhood-by-neighborhood systems)

–internal financing is a key goal to an organization so heavily involved in politics; ACORN would like to be totally financed by those who are benefiting from the organization (membership dues and internal fund raising)

–because ACORN is a geographically based organization, members belong to an ACORN neighborhood or community affiliate rather than to this or that issue-oriented committee; the idea is that low to moderate income citizens must be organized, be committed to a permanent organization that will attack the maldistribution of power across the board over the long run

• "An organization created in a neighborhood rather than in response to a particular issue is, by its very definition, an organization which transcends this or that issue and which takes on importance in and of itself."

Structure

• a membership democracy with 3 separate and distinct components: membership, leadership, staff

• membership: 36,000 families in 23 states; each member belongs to a neighborhood group

• leadership: governed by the elected leadership of the neighborhood organizations; 1 representative from each ACORN neighborhood group sits on local and state executive boards; ACORN's national policy-making body, the Association Board, consists of two elected representatives from each ACORN state

- staff: staff numbered 167 in 1979 with starting salary of $3,600/year; staff is fairly evenly divided between male and female—9 of the 19 Head Organizers are women

Funding

- breakdown of 1979 operating budget of 1.6 million according to source:
    - -37.4% internal financing (primarily dues of $16 per family per year)
    - -24.7% church funded (largest outside contributor the Campaign for Human Development)
    - -24% government funded (primarily through VISTA)
    - -13.9% foundation funded (almost entirely for expansion and campaigns on specific issues)

- each state is responsible for generating its own budget through a combination of internal and external fund-raising; each state contributes a small percentage to the core budget of the association

Organizing/Action Methodologies

- initial linchpin of new ACORNs is the organizer (staff)

- organizers are skilled professionals trained at the Arkansas Institute for Social Justice

- organizers are responsible for putting together an organized drive in an unorganized neighborhood and over a period of 6 weeks seeing to it that a new local ACORN group is formed

- organizing drive begins when ACORN is invited into a neighborhood by some of its residents or the Executive Board picks a neighborhood to be organized (for various strategic reasons)

- unions and churches have helped ACORN with initial neighborhood contacts

- the organizer does not build coalitions of existing organizations; each new ACORN group is created from scratch

- the organizer molds initial contacts into an organizing committee, typically 10-20 couples in a neighborhood of 1,000 homes

- the organizing committee, with the organizer's assistance, develops a set of issues they feel will strike responsive chords in their neighborhood

- the ability of the organizing committee to create an effective local group depends to a great extent on their own understanding of the necessity of creating such an organization

- once the initial agenda of issues has been developed, the organizer and the organizing committee begin systematically to contact everyone in the neighborhood; this door to door work takes about a month and leads up to the first meeting of the new local group

- veteran ACORN members or leaders from other groups attend the first meeting to talk about what ACORN is doing elsewhere in the city and state; the organizing committee sets out tentative plans for dealing with the issues which have emerged; people are asked to join, temporary officers are elected and the group is in existence

- all along, the organizer is responsible for working with the group in helping them develop campaigns, issues, tactics and strategies, acting as liaison between the local membership/leadership and the organization's support staff in New Orleans; the organizer arranges for support staff to lend technical or legal assistance or research; the organizer works with the Executive Board in his or her region or city on the development of regional and city-wide plans and directions necessary to local success:
  (a) educating members and leadership on principles of organizing and tactics
  (b) focusing on direct organizing and actions (instead of social service)
  (c) professionalizing organizing (instead of personalizing it)
  (d) developing a plan for organizational self-sufficiency
  (e) having statistical criteria for evaluation of situations/actions

Examples of Activities

- hard-hitting actions on ArkLa Gas headquarters in Little Rock resulted in new rules on shut-offs from the Public Service Commission

- ACORN anti-inflation campaign demands that corporations pledge to comply with voluntary price guidelines; actions in 20 cities on oil company headquarters, gas stations and supermarkets

- Colorado ACORN negotiated a strong shut-off policy from the Public Service Company

- ACORN actions in Star City, Arkansas, forced a laundromat owner to remove a "Whites Only" sign and admit blacks

- Sioux Falls ACORN members won free bus service for school children

- Carolina Action/ACORN won citywide referendum in Greensboro on election of school board members by district

- Memphis ACORN blocked demolition of the city's only public hospital

- in response to Georgia/ACORN pressure, Georgia Public Service Commission adopted experimental Lifeline telephone rates

- Des Moines ACORN scuttled plans to use $8.5 million in public money for a downtown parking garage

- Memphis ACORN got Drexel Chemical Company to agree to stop producing toxic chemicals at a plant in the ACORN neighborhood

- Carolina Action/ACORN won first Nuclear Regulatory Commission ruling banning transport of nuclear waste through Charlotte

- Detroit ACORN demanded that public money being spent on the 1980 Republican National Convention be matched with funds for neighborhood improvements

- Philadelphia ACORN members began squatting in abandoned houses to force the city to clean up administration of its Gift Property program

- in response to ACORN pressure, Philadelphia water commissioner lowers residential rates

- CAL/ACORN beat an attempt to repeal Lifeline utility rates in the California state legislature

- Austin City Council rejected Overall Economic Development Plan after ACORN protested over displacement of low and moderate income people and lack of citizen input

- Tulsa ACORN filed formal complaint with HUD against the city's Community Development Block Grant proposal and held its own public hearing attended by 100 members and HUD officials

- Arizona Public Service agreed to negotiate with ACORN to head off a challenge of its franchise renewal with the city

- ACORN members in Davenport and St. Louis personally delivered the People's Platform to President Carter

- 2500 Laclede Gas customers in St. Louis began withholding payment of utility bills and demanded a rebate of money the company would save during a gas workers' strike

- WMNF, a non-commercial FM radio station affiliated with ACORN, was established in Tampa, Florida

- Georgia Action/ACORN beat a ballot referendum to increase the sales tax in Atlanta

- the Federal Reserve Board ruled that Landmark Central could not acquire a suburban bank until a joint agreement on community reinvestment was reached with a St. Louis ACORN

Associated Organizations

ACORN has helped establish a number of organizations which complement and assist ACORN's work. Among these—

• The Institute for Social Justice, a national training and research center; with offices in New Orleans, Boston and Little Rock, the Institute offers a variety of training programs and on-site consultations to other community organizations; the Institute also publishes the bi-monthly magazine, *Just Economics*, and organizing handbooks; in addition, the Institute accepts and administers tax exempt funds earmarked for ACORN's research and educational work

• Associated Media Foundation Movement (AM/FM), set up by ACORN in 1977 to begin developing a network of non-commercial radio stations in ACORN cities to give low and moderate income people access to the airwaves

• United Labor Organizations (ULO), initiated at the direction of the Association Board and now the organizing component of the National Center for Jobs and Justice campaign to represent the interests of unemployed and underemployed workers; ULO organizing is underway in Detroit, Philadelphia, Boston and New Orleans

• ACORN Political Action Committee (APAC), an independent organization (with a structure parallel to ACORN's) which interviews, endorses and works for candidates for elected office; through APAC, ACORN members themselves have been elected to a number of city councils, school boards and other local offices

NATIONAL ASSOCIATION OF NEIGHBORHOODS (N.A.N.)
1651 Fuller Street, N.W., Washington, D.C. 20009, 202-332-7766

The N.A.N. is a membership organization of neighborhood organizations from around the country which are involved in the struggle of low income neighborhoods to revitalize (without displacement)

History

In 1975 over 100 neighborhood leaders from 5 cities met to discuss common issues and problems; they formed the Alliance for Neighborhood Government, now the N.A.N., to continue coordination of efforts and to expand communication among neighborhoods across the country

N.A.N. has expanded to a membership of 500 neighborhood coalitions and organizations as well as numerous individual members

Philosophy/Goals

• to encourage productive reindustrializing use of public/private dollars in urban revitalization (as opposed to speculative use)

- to advocate in Washington for neighborhood groups all over America
- to assist low income neighborhoods to revitalize without displacement
- to support neighborhood empowerment through neighborhood government
- to encourage respect for diversity in neighborhoods
- to support interdependence, inter-neighborhood decision and action
- the N.A.N.'s Neighborhood Bill of Responsibilities and Rights asserts that all governments and private institutions must recognize:
  - the right of neighborhoods to determine their own goals, consistent with the broad civic ideals of justice and human equality
  - the right of neighborhoods to define their own governing structures, operating procedures, names and boundaries
  - the right of democratically organized neighborhoods to control private and public resources necessary for the implementation and support of neighborhood decisions
  - the right of democratically organized neighborhoods to review in advance and decisively influence all stages of planning and implementation of all actions of government and private institutions affecting the neighborhood
  - the right of neighborhoods to information necessary to carry out these rights

Structure

- N.A.N. is a membership organization
- overseeing N.A.N. activities is a large national Board with 7 regional vice presidents, a secretary and a treasurer
- a small Board oversees the work of the National Action Coalition of N.A.N.
- N.A.N.'s Executive Director and staff in Washington coordinate the organization's activities

Funding

- future funding may depend somewhat less on the government and somewhat more on corporation foundation grants
- traditional sources of approximately $425,000 in annual expenditures have been:
  - government (National VISTA Sponsor Grant, EPA, e.g.)
  - foundations
  - memberships ($65/yr./organizations, $25/yr./individuals)
  - subscriptions, publications, conferences

**Organizing/Action Methodologies—
Examples of Activities**

- *National Displacement Project*
  - under a National VISTA Sponsor Grant N.A.N. has placed 45 volunteer neighborhood organizers with 22 neighborhood organizations in 12 cities
  - N.A.N. publishes a bi-monthly newsletter on displacement which is disseminated to 2,000 organizations
  - ACTION funded N.A.N.'s development of a Handbook on Anti-Displacement Strategies
  - research is conducted on issues associated with anti-displacement (such as residential stability and lifetime tenancy)
  - a training format has been developed which centers around displacement
  - N.A.N. has worked to build coalitions between churches and neighborhood organizations on the displacement issue
  - above resources are funneled into the local VISTA project organizations to help support and maintain displacement prevention efforts of groups

- local successes of the National Displacement Project include
  - United Tenants of Albany (Albany, New York) succeeded in getting the county to implement a program in which tenants can purchase, in advance of auction, county-owned, tax-foreclosed buildings;
  - Fremont Public Association (Seattle, Washington) organized tenants in half of the neighborhood's residential buildings, and established a successful coalition between tenants and the neighborhood's home-owners through a local Community Council;
  - Children and Youth Development Service (Brooklyn, New York) established a program, with the local Community Board and Police Department, to seal off and provide surveillance to abandoned, arson-prone buildings; a program is now being developed to purchase and renovate these buildings;
  - Adams Morgan Organization (Washington, D.C.) avoided displacement of tenants from a building and then convinced the city to purchase the building for public housing, allowing the tenants to remain; established tenant workshops and a housing counseling service to help tenants stay in their buildings through purchase;
  - ESHAC (Milwaukee, Wisconsin) established a neighborhood real estate brokerage firm which purchases and rehabilitates absentee-owned properties and sells them to low and moderate income families currently living in the neighborhood;
  - Cedar Riverside Project Area Committee (Minneapolis, Minnesota) successfully stopped HUD from foreclosing on a large Section 236-funded housing complex; the organization is now

helping the tenants to negotiate for purchase of this building, with financial assistance from HUD and the current owners

- *Quiet Neighborhood Self-Help Project*, a joint effort of N.A.N. and the U.S. Environmental Protection Agency's Office of Noise Abatement and Control
    - provides technical information and organizing strategies to numerous neighborhood organizations that are confronting specific noise problems
    - targets assistance to a select number of groups
    - developed a national network of neighborhood organizations involved in noise control

- specific efforts of the Quiet Neighborhood Self-Help Project include
    - assistance to neighborhood organizations in monitoring noise problems, negotiating directly with the sources creating the noise, making noise control ordinances more relevant and enforceable
    - establishing Neighborhood Noise Information Centers
    - bringing together neighborhood organizations, local elected and noise control officials, businesses, industries, and others to Neighborhood Noise Control Workshops
    - publishing the *Quiet Neighborhoods* newsletter
    - establishing a demonstration Environmental Organizing Project which provides VISTA volunteers to selected neighborhood organizations working on noise and related environmental problems
    - development of an organizing Guide for the Quiet Neighborhood Self-Help Project which provides an overview of the organizing process so that a neighborhood organization will have the organizational strength and ability to utilize the techniques for abating airport, highway and "neighborhood" noise

- *N.A.N. Neighborhood Training School*
    - trains citizen leaders of neighborhood organizations
    - offers workshops covering such topics as lobbying, displacement prevention strategies, delivery of family and youth services

- *Neighborhood Action Coalition*
    - chief goal is to implement the National Neighborhood Platform which was adopted in 1979
    - held press conferences in 5 cities in 1980 to announce the platform
    - organized meetings with the presidential candidates to question them on their support for the platform
    - testified at the Democratic Party Platform Committee Hearing and held conferences with the Republican and Citizen Party

Platform Committee members which resulted in all three parties having platform planks on neighborhoods for the first time
–lobbies in Washington with regard to issues such as neighborhood empowerment, housing displacement, and youth employment; provides testimony before congressional committees on these issues
–marshals N.A.N. membership to contact congressmen for key votes on N.A.N.'s principal issues
–developed testimony on "Neighborhoods in the 1980s" for the Reuss Subcommittee on the Cities
–tabulated a congressional neighborhood voting record
–supported Rep. Henry B. Gonzalez to chair the House Subcommittee on Housing and Community Development (of the Committee on Banking, Finance and Urban Affairs) during the current Congress (Rep. Gonzalez was elected)

OPPORTUNITIES INDUSTRIALIZATION CENTERS OF AMERICA (OIC/A) 100 W. Coulter Street, Philadelphia, Pennsylvania 19144, 215-849-3010

"A network of comprehensive employment training and community development programs (OICs) across the nation"

History

Founded in Philadelphia in 1964 by Rev. Leon Sullivan OIC/A has grown into a national technical assistance organization which serves local OICs in 130 cities in 42 states, Washington, D.C., and the U.S. Virgin Islands

Over the years local OICs with the assistance of OIC/A have trained over 640,000 persons, approximately 79% of whom have gotten jobs

Philosophy/Goals

• to serve disadvantaged and underskilled Americans of all races in the areas of employment and training, alternative education systems, community economic development, housing for the aged, urban revitalization

• to provide channels for low income people to create and operate neighborhood economies, assuring that skills and needed education are available, creating income through the earnings of job holders, creating jobs in the community, providing opportunities for modest capital accumulation, investing in sound, income-generating ventures within the community, creating an ever-expanding economic impact area

- fundamental task: training and placing America's poor and disadvantaged citizens in productive permanent jobs
- self-help is the central organizing principle
    - in program administration: competing for contracts, developing independent sources of revenue, creatively meeting community needs
    - in each program: self-sufficient earners through job training excellence, self-determining communities through creation of ownership and cooperative vehicles to exercise leadership and organization involvement
    - as the underlying objective of every relationship and service: emphasizing the spirit of collaboration and mutual respect that ensures progress amid diversity, creating a national self-help system of Americans working together to strengthen our nation

Structure

- in addition to the national office and 9 regional offices, as of 1980 there were 144 funded OIC affiliates and 60 groups interested in starting OICs in their communities
- a combined staff of nearly 5,000 men and women work at the national and local levels
- policy and over-all direction at each affiliate is set by a volunteer board of directors, in relation to the mandates for all OICs contained in the OIC/A Affiliate Agreement
- OIC/A regional staff (in 9 regional offices) assist local boards through preparation of special reports on local, regional and national activities and perform various other services
- a variety of training is offered to local boards through the Management Training School of the Opportunities Academy of Management Training (OAMT) (an independent non-profit training organization providing staff development services to a wide variety of agencies and organizations involved in human resource development)
- leadership training is also provided by the Leadership Development unit of OAMT for boards of directors, executive directors and OIC interest groups; the training emphasizes community involvement, corporate support, individual initiative, and basic economics
- the Management Training School of OAMT also provides management skill training for staff and boards
- OICs are responsible to the communities they serve, to their boards of directors, and to their funding sources

Funding

- by the end of 1980 OICs were competing for and independently managing over $100 million in program funds from diverse sources—corporations, government (federal, state, and local), foundations, individuals

- major corporations donated nearly $5 million in 1980

- OICs receive funds from the U.S. Department of Labor through CETA; projects are also funded by the U.S. Departments of Commerce and Education

- most affiliates receive their operating funds through CETA

- per student, OIC costs approximately 1/3 as much as government manpower programs

Organizing/Action Methodologies

- OICs are established as a result of: community people writing to OIC offices and expressing interest; prime sponsors inviting OIC/A to identify potential initiators in their area (because the prime sponsor feels OIC may enhance local programming); or industry, after hearing of OIC sucess in other areas, asking for help in getting an OIC started

- an Interest Group is formed and tries to involve the right mix of community representatives, elects a Board of Directors, becomes affiliated with OIC/A, does a feasibility study and develops a proposal for funding; OIC/A regional offices provide crucial help along the way; representatives of the Interest Group are sent to Philadelphia for National Orientation

- the local OIC, when a significant new job field is found to be developing locally, will try to develop a related training course

- to develop an area of training, a local company may be asked to lend an instructor to teach the new course; a regional office fiscal specialist may review the proposed budget; the OIC/A Resource Center may provide the relevant curriculum materials; the regional office may become involved in negotiations with the CETA prime sponsors, helping to integrate the proposed new program with the area's overall training plans

- the comprehensive OIC model includes: recruitment, intake, orientation, counseling, supportive service, "Feeder" training (which prepares the disadvantaged for job training through a combination of basic education, "world of work" courses, minority history and related subjects), job development, job placement, and follow-up

- OIC/A helps affiliates become comprehensive by giving assistance in negotiating contracts, proposal development, evaluation of existing services, developing local awareness of the need for comprehensive OIC services, or finding alternative funding for program components

- an annual convocation, regional conferences, workshops, and planning conferences all help in training (sessions include such topics as counseling, fiscal procedures, other aspects of operating and improving an OIC)

- support groups such as auxiliaries, clergy committees, and alumni associations have been an important force in OIC/A technical assistance; it is a goal for every OIC to have all three groups or be working to establish them

Examples of Activities

- OIC/A established model alternative high schools to help dropouts and potential dropouts; these Career Intern Programs (CIPs) are operating in Philadelphia, Seattle, Detroit, New York City and Poughkeepsie, New York

- OIC/A Division of Special Programs provides technical assistance to OICs in seven cities operating summer Career Exploration Programs (CEPs); CEPs enable disadvantaged youth to explore careers both at various workplaces and in the classroom

- the Hudson Valley OIC in Poughkeepsie, New York operates a program serving the handicapped; through its Skills Discovery Center, the handicapped find their natural abilities and interests; adult basic education, counseling and training services are available; placement rate after 90 days in the program is 55% (compared with the national rate in the 24-33% range)

- in Philadelphia, a special OIC branch known as the Antonini Center serves many Hispanic people

- the Philadelphia OIC also serves delinquent youth through a system of three group homes, residential facilities which serve as alternatives to institutionalization; in addition, the Community Advocate Program of the Philadelphia OIC provides counseling intervention for troubled youth

- the OIC of Greater Boston helps many recent immigrants to this country with an English as a Second Language Program; after learning practical, conversational speaking skills, and acquiring a basic reading ability in English, students may go on to a variety of skills training courses (similar courses are available at many OICs across the country)

- the Green Giant Company gave an $11,000 grant to the Rio Grande OIC in Weslaco, Texas, for an evening employability program serving migrant farm workers (Green Giant, concerned that its program of agricultural mechanization might leave some farm workers jobless, took this step to assist in providing pre-vocational courses to make it possible for the farm workers to learn saleable skills leading to good jobs)

- at the OIC in Providence, Rhode Island, control systems for jet engine aircraft and environmental data systems for wide-body airplanes are being built; annual gross sales are approximately $1 million

- the OIC in Pittsburgh is matching potential purchasers with houses, helping them get mortgages, and rehabilitating the structures; OIC received a $75,000 contract to perform this service from the Pennsylvania Community Affairs Office and the local Urban Redevelopment Authority; under the program, labor costs are free to home buyers

- the New Orleans OIC has trained eight trainees to provide weatherization and minor repairs to homes owned by handicapped, elderly, and low-income persons

- the Colorado OIC in Denver was assisted by the OIC/A Region VI Office in developing a clerical training program

- the OIC/A Region II office evaluated Adult Basic Education materials from various companies and is developing an annotated bibliography for OICs; when complete, affiliates wanting to start Adult Basic Education components will be spared some initial research involved in evaluating different types of learning materials

- the Region VII office helped the St. Louis OIC to replicate a successful Career Assessment Exploration Center (CEAC) in operation at the Kansas City, Missouri OIC; regional office support was offered at meetings with the CETA prime sponsor and with the provider of the CEAC materials; through this funded program the disadvantaged of St. Louis can get hands-on experience at the OIC in plumbing, electronics, and several other job clusters

Individual Projects/Groups: A Sampler

BILINGUAL COMMUNITY RADIO STATION PROJECT
P.O. Box 1243, Salinas, California 93902, 408-757-8039

Focus

media/training

Nature of Group

bilingual community radio station, urban and rural

Project/Group Description

- KUBO/Voces Unidas broadcasts in Monterey and Santa Cruz counties in California; it is the only public radio facility in Salinas and the only medium providing educational, informational and cultural programs in Spanish and English for the 450,000 residents of the two counties served

- a goal of the project is to help the Spanish-speaking population to build a positive self-image through active participation in programming

- another emphasis is on training in all aspects of radio

Funding

- Corporation for Public Broadcasting
- Public Communications Facilities Program
- CETA

- Campaign for Human Development
- Hewlett Foundation

Project/Group Structure

- 11 paid staff members
- 40 volunteers (sources of volunteers: recruited from public meetings, schools, volunteer organizations, neighborhood meetings, public announcements over the station)
- Voces Unidas Bilingual Broadcasting Foundation was established as a tax-exempt non-profit corporation to operate KUBO; the foundation holds the license for the station granted by the Federal Communications Commission and is the grantee for all funds going to the station
- current Foundation structure includes:
  -9 member Board of Directors elected by the membership of the Foundation (Foundation membership granted to all people who contribute money or volunteer time to the station)
- a community advisory committee was also established to advise the Foundation Board and station staff on programs aired by KUBO
- the station must fit its structure to the laws governing non-profit corporations in California (as these change)

Methods That Have Worked

- since the station is newly on the air, many of the structures and ideas are just being tested

Methods to Avoid/Cautions

- since funding is changing dramatically for public media, old methods of financing will not work within the next few years; new groups starting stations should carefully look at old models to see if past start-up resources in fact still exist

Role of Religious Institutions, the Gospel, Liturgy, in Project/Group Functioning:

- partial funding

CITIZENS LEAGUE OF WOONSOCKET TOGETHER (CLOWT)
P.O. Box 694, Woonsocket, Rhode Island 02895, 401-767-3582

Focus

neighborhood organizing/empowerment

Nature of Group

local non-profit in urban area

Project/Group Description

• multi-issue, multi-ethnic grassroots community organization

• dedicated to involving low-income and working-class residents in resolving social problems confronting them in their lives (e.g., transportation, vandalism, deteriorating housing, low quality education)

• democratically controlled

Funding

• Campaign for Human Development

• Mott Foundation

• Sisters of Mercy

• local fund raising

• other foundations and private grants

Project/Group Structure

• 5½ paid staff members

• over 500 volunteers (sources of volunteers: door knocking, neighborhood meetings, networking of groups and organizations)

• via Community Congress, 17 members of the Board of Directors are elected; key priority issues also result from this process

• participants develop block clubs and neighborhood associations which democratically define and address issues

Methods That Have Worked

• door knocking; working on the issues raised by the process of door knocking

• empowering people to plan and chair meetings with invited guests

• the power of *numbers* holds a guest responsible to the group; by increasing the participation in public forum meetings, the residents have become known as a power for change previously underutilized

• success breeding success—provide for victories by the "cutting" of issues

• keeping meetings in *their* neighborhoods

• networking of people from neighborhood groups and city organizations to provide a momentum and effectiveness for the city-wide Community Congress and for issues that lend themselves to coalition-building for resolutions

Methods To Avoid/Cautions

• staff determining what issues people *should* be concerned about

• staff must avoid viewing their jobs as regular jobs with regular working hours; near total availability is needed

• individuals making decisions for a group without consulting other members—the group is no one person's group

Role of Religious Institutions, the Gospel, Liturgy, in Project/Group Functioning

• partial funding

• the group is involved in action on behalf of justice and participation in the transformation of the world—both "constitutive dimensions of the preaching of the gospel" (1979 Bishops' Synod)

COMMISSION ON CATHOLIC COMMUNITY ACTION (CCCA)
1027 Superior Avenue, Cleveland, Ohio 44114, 216-696-6525

Focus

community action

Nature of Group

diocese-connected in metropolitan area

Project/Group Description

• CCCA is one of the largest diocesan social action offices in the United States

• functions as a catalyst within communities by soliciting interest and inciting the enthusiasm of all people to eradicate social and economic injustice, solve social problems, and promote equality and human dignity

• the Commission functions in both adversary and advocacy roles in trying to shape and reshape organizations and institutions to make them serve human beings rather than oppress them

• the Commission traditionally has focused on four basic categories of activity: education, issues, community development, allocations

• *Education* (activities *include*):
  - *Social Justice Education Task Force*
  - *Commission Action Network*, a monthly legislative bulletin
  - support for the Akron Catholic Commission
  - frequent issue lectures at St. Mary's (diocesan) seminary
  - monthly involvement in the diocese's Continuing Education for Priests

- *Issues* (activities *include*):
  - *Housing Task Force*—improves housing conditions for lower income persons and promotes integrated living patterns
  - *Criminal Justice Task Force*—organized opposition to reinstatement of capital punishment in Ohio; works on state prison reform with emphasis on local alternatives to incarceration; monitors local jails, public defender's office and judicial system; is involved in the search for a solution to both crime and inhumanity
  - *Full Employment Task Force*—monitors and helps shape manpower planning in the community by participating locally with the CETA Consortium and the County Overall Economic Development Plan Board; encourages parish-based self-help projects to identify, convene, and empower the unemployed in Cleveland neighborhoods; participated in various national efforts to successfully pass the Humphrey-Hawkins Full Employment Act
  - *Health Care Task Force*—responds to the issues of access for the poor to health care delivery, specifically to the growing dilemma of hospitals planning to leave the inner city and relocate in the suburbs
  - *Welfare Reform*—Commission is an active member of the "Campaign for Children," a coalition of church groups and community organizations advocating for increased AFDC welfare grants (tools include testimony, telegrams, letters and personal contact with legislators); welfare reform is an ongoing priority, but activity increases when the state budget is being developed and again when the biannual budget is adjusted
  - *Spanish Community Development Task Force*—monitors Cleveland's Bilingual Education Program; active on the Board of Education's Law Compliance Advisory Board; was a key factor in organizing the Hispanic Coalition for Peaceful Desegregation and Bilingual Education (a coalition comprised of 35 organizations and 150 members); was instrumental in the creation of a parish neighborhood organizing project involving redlining
  - *Bishop's Committee on School Desegregation*—although not a Commission Task Force, this committee is located in CCCA's office and works in conjunction with CCCA staff

- *Community Development* (activities *include*):
  - *Training and Technical Assistance Project*—recruits and trains new neighborhood staff organizers; conducts ongoing skill building sessions for existing staff and/or weekly consultations with neighborhood staff Directors, specially tailored leadership development seminars conducted regularly for each organization; offers focused technical assistance ranging from funding and proposals help to securing and scheduling consultants with special expertise for quality research on city-wide issues

- *Allocations* (activities *include*):
  - managing the Campaign for Human Development's annual collection and distributing/monitoring the local 25% share remaining in

the diocese (which is allocated to self-help community groups)
–administering the Catholic Hunger Fund which maintains 22 Crisis Hunger Centers in 4 counties

Funding

• Catholic Charities Corporation provides the core operating budget for the Commission

• the Commission secures more than $1 million annually from government and philanthropic sources to support many neighborhood organizations, special-issue research, and advocacy programs

Project/Group Structure

• 15 paid staff members

• many individual volunteers associated with the Task Forces and projects of the Commission

• an elected Commission of fifty members which develops policies, shapes action strategies, and participates in implementation

• the Commission is an active member of the diocesan system and receives helpful support from the Bishop and his Secretary for Social Concerns

• the Commission's chairman is a member of the Executive Committee of the Federation of Catholic Community Services, and its staff participates in Social Concerns Secretariat meetings as well as in the FCCS Council of Executives

• many Commission members serve on the Diocesan Pastoral Council in addition to other diocesan organizations and institutions

• the Commission's Executive Director serves on the Diocesan Board of Consultants

Methods That Have Worked

• those which foster community organizations which are open and democratic, resident-controlled, action-oriented and value centered

• those which foster the dignity of the human person, true autonomy and self-determination

Role of Religious Institutions, the Gospel, Liturgy, in Project/Group Functioning:

• CCCA is the official social action agent of the Catholic Diocese of Cleveland

• partial funding

• Commission's rationale for supporting neighborhood organizations:
  (1) it is in the best interests of our church, because the future of each

parish is directly dependent upon the future of its neighborhoods and the quality of life for those who live there;

(2) it is in keeping with our church's teaching that actions for justice are a constitutive element of preaching the Gospel;

(3) it is essential to our shared ministry that we act to motivate, to energize, to enable, and community organization continues to prove itself as a positive vehicle for the empowerment of people and the development of their leadership abilities

CONSUMER HEALTH ACCESS GROUP PROJECT (parent organization: Consumer Coalition for Health)
P.O. Box 50088, Washington, D.C. 20004, 202-638-5828

Focus

health

Nature of Group

national coalition of religious, civil rights, labor, senior citizens, women's and civic groups

Project/Group Description

• provides technical assistance, training, and political advice/support to low-income community organizations working on equal access to health care for minorities and the poor (includes fighting cutbacks)

• provides some administrative/legislative advocacy in Washington but is essentially a grass-roots oriented group serving the staff and volunteers of 36 different groups in their own communities

• holds regional conferences to strengthen local organizing efforts

• produced a comprehensive guidebook geared to helping communities overcome health care barriers

• established a national monitoring project to tract down illegal cutbacks or discriminatory implementation of federally funded health care programs

Funding

• memberships

• private donations

• small amounts from unions and church groups

• Campaign for Human Development

Project/Group Structure

• 1.5 paid staff members

- volunteers: equivalent of 1 fulltime (sources of volunteers: interested advocates salted away in government, universities or the health care delivery system)

- the Board is composed 2/3 of local activists, 1/3 of representatives of national organizations

- very loose-knit structure

Methods That Have Worked

- direct action

- creative use of planning and regulatory processes

- participation (creation) of broad-based coalitions

Methods to Avoid/Cautions

- beware of being tagged as a "poor people's group"—it isolates you

- try to find workers, professionals, even service providers with interests allied to yours on a single issue, and work with (through) them: unless you are a *very* strong grass-roots group, peddling influence is better than having none

Role of Religious Institutions, the Gospel, Liturgy, in Project/Group Functioning:

- partial funding

- "Pray for the dead, and fight like hell for the living!"

DRUG STORE ACQUISITION PROJECT (parent organization: West Bank Community Development Corporation, Inc.)
2000 S. 5th Street, Minneapolis, Minnesota 55454, 612-376-1092

Focus

economic development

Nature of Group

neighborhood-connected in urban area

Project/Group Description

- the West Bank Coop Pharmacy—offers prescription drugs, health and beauty aids, vitamins, cards, film, some appliances, school and office supplies, medical equipment, some household items

- the business was purchased by the West Bank Coop Grocery as a second division with the West Bank Community Development Corporation acting as the parent organization

- the drug store is located in the Cedar-Riverside Urban Renewal Area, which is being redeveloped to benefit the low and moderate income population

Funding

- Campaign for Human Development Economic Development Loan ($40,000 at 0% for 8 years)
- Community Development Corporation Loan ($30,000 at 10.75% for 8 years)
- private bank financing ($40,000)
- private individual loan ($56,000)

Project/Group Structure

- 12 paid staff members
- 0 volunteers (the nature of the business—drug sales—prohibits the use of volunteer labor)
- during the first year the store was managed by a worker collective; the Board of Directors is moving to install a more structured management, using one key management position, with the collective participating in decisions

Methods That Have Worked

- a high degree of skill and experience is needed for key management positions
- collective management is something that needs to be *phased in*

Methods to Avoid/Cautions

- loose collective management
- having a management not firmly under the control of a board
- lack of effective communication between the board and the staff—this is critical in order to avoid problems piling up to crisis proportions

Role of Religious Institutions, the Gospel, Liturgy, in Project/Group Functioning:

- partial funding
- a strong humanitarian feeling exists among members of board and staff which is directed to the customers and the neighborhood at large

FORDHAM BEDFORD HOUSING CORPORATION
2656 Decatur Avenue, Bronx, New York 10458, 212-367-3200

Focus

housing

Nature of Group

neighborhood organization in urban area

Project/Group Description

• a not-for-profit corporation with the goal of maintaining sound housing in their neighborhood

• major objective is to avoid abandonment and seek improvements for the valuable housing stock in the neighborhood

• FBHC currently manages 4 area apartment buildings and provides technical assistance to tenants and managers in 7 other buildings

• FBHC is providing community input for the rehabilitation project proposed for 4 vacant buildings

• FBHC is meeting with city housing and finance officials to develop a plan for proper handling of future buildings taken for tax liens

• FBHC is working with a government Neighborhood Preservation Program on Interim Site Improvements for several vacant areas

Funding

• CETA Title VI

• Campaign for Human Development (funds management assistance)

• local banks and corporations

• (FBHC is receiving technical assistance from the Council of New York Law Associates and the Volunteer Urban Consulting Group)

Project/Group Structure

• 6 paid staff members (5 of 6 are local residents)

• 35 volunteers (sources of volunteers: tenant and block associations, local institutions, Fordham Bedford Community Coalition)

• Board of Directors (all local residents)

• FBHC is a not-for-profit 501 (c) 3 corporation with federal and state tax exemption

Methods That Have Worked

• working with an organized group of tenants

• tenants participating directly in decision-making

• tenants pushing for improvements

• coordination of available private and public reinvestment funds

Role of Religious Institutions, the Gospel, Liturgy, in Project/Group Functioning:

• partial funding

IOWA ACORN ORGANIZING PROJECT
Insurance Exchange Building, 2nd and Pershing, Davenport, Iowa 52801, 319-322-6176

Focus

community organizing

Nature of Group

neighborhood-connected, urban and rural

Project/Group Description

- a community organization working on neighborhood, city, and national issues—energy/utility issues, taxes, Community Development Block Grant funding, housing

Funding

- Campaign for Human Development
- internal

Project/Group Structure

- 2 paid staff members (1 in Davenport, 1 in Des Moines)
- ACORN member volunteers
- 14 neighborhood groups in 2 cities

Methods That Have Worked

(see Organizing/Action methodologies section of the ACORN national profile in Section II)

- direct action methods have proved effective

Methods to Avoid/Cautions

- staff advocacy
- service-oriented programs

Role of Religious Institutions, the Gospel, Liturgy, in Project/Group Functioning:

- partial funding
- many meetings held in churches
- ACORN works well with churches as part of the community

43

ST. LOUIS ASSOCIATION OF COMMUNITY ORGANIZATIONS (SLACO) 608 N. Spring, St. Louis, Missouri 63108

Focus

multi-issue/community organization

Nature of Group

neighborhood-based in urban area

Project/Group Description

- a coalition of 7 neighborhood groups in all-black, low-moderate income areas
- each group works on local issues facing its own community
- the 7 groups join forces to address the broader issues facing all the neighborhoods (e.g., housing, inadequate city services, insensitive expenditure of CDBG funds)

Funding

- Campaign for Human Development
- other foundation grants
- corporations
- religious communities
- community fund-raisers

Project/Group Structure

- 5 paid staff members (Director, 1 office staff person, remainder are organizers)
- 3 (fulltime) volunteers (source of volunteers: VISTA—expires in March, 1982)
- a Sponsoring Committee was formed in 1978 to establish the organization; Board of Directors was elected from the Sponsoring Committee

Methods That Have Worked

- a commitment to working on local agendas set by local people themselves
- a commitment to the development of strong, skilled local leadership
- good training, direction and cooperation of staff
- involvement of as many people as possible in all areas of organization: issue identification, research, strategy development, outreach to neighbors and local institutions

- maintenance of good lines of communication within the organization, and with the other components of the community—churches, businesses, schools, etc.

- good, solid preparation—research and planning strategies for all issues, and for the growth of the organization

- keeping the focus on issues in the community rather than personalities, politics

- taking people where they are; making sure they help develop all strategies and are comfortable with actions taken by the group

- keeping the purpose of organizing in front of you at all times: to affect change for justice through the empowerment of people, to bring dignity and hope to individuals and communities

Methods to Avoid/Cautions

- *avoid cookbook organizing*: recognize that each community, and each opponent is different; what worked in another city may not work in your city; what worked in your city five years ago may not work today; as community organizing becomes more widespread, our opponents are becoming more sophisticated and more callous—community organizations must face the challenge by becoming more sophisticated and more skilled

- a top heavy group with heavy influence of staff and a handful of "leaders" with little or no base, therefore no organization, no empowerment, no accountability

- inexperienced, poorly trained and directed staff

- loss of independence through political deals, etc.

- poor planning, shoddy research, no direction = no action, no long term change

- isolation from other bases of power and influence in the community

Role of Religious Institutions, the Gospel, Liturgy, in Project/Group Functioning:

- partial funding

- endorsed by the Catholic Archdiocese of St. Louis

- the inception of SLACO and the continuing organizing efforts are in direct response to the Gospel mandate for action on behalf of justice

- people make a point of opening all meetings with prayer

- people involved with SLACO place a high priority on involving their churches in the work of the neighborhoods

UTILITY SERVICE ADVOCACY PROJECT (parent organization: Pennsylvania Alliance for Jobs and Energy)
111 Smithfield Street, Pittsburgh, Pennsylvania 15222,
412-566-2290

Focus

energy

Nature of Group

alliance of 8 neighborhood groups, urban and rural

Project/Group Description

- democratic, grassroots, action-oriented organization

- dedicated to create changes in the regulations and policies of energy companies and regulatory agencies (e.g., obtaining a delay in a rate increase requested by a utility and a postponement in billing dates)

Funding

- Campaign for Human Development
- CETA
- ACTION
- State of Pennsylvania
- door-to-door canvas

Project/Group Structure

- 15 paid staff members
- volunteer hours 1980-81: 4,000 (sources of volunteers: members and member groups)

Methods That Have Worked

- door-to-door canvas
- large actions
- public pressure on government officials

Methods to Avoid/Cautions

- attempting to stop *total* rate hikes; focus on *reducing* rates
- avoid protracted legal and legislative fights

Role of Religious Institutions, the Gospel, Liturgy, in Project/Group Functioning:

- a basis of the project is the need for social justice in energy pricing as well as the proper stewardship of the earth's resources

WEST OAKLAND FOOD PROJECT, INC.
925 W. Grand Avenue, Oakland, California 94607, 415-834-5854

Focus

economic development/health and nutrition

Nature of Group

community group in urban area

Project/Group Description

• a locally organized campaign to address the high unemployment rate of youth in West Oakland, to address the inner city food needs of West Oakland, and to address the need to establish an economic base through residents of West Oakland owning membership shares in economic ventures

• the project works to establish links between inner city consumers and rural producer co-ops and to educate the West Oakland community about cooperative principles

• the group established and operates a co-op grocery store in West Oakland

• further plans include purchase of the entire commercial block in which the food co-op is located, the development of a co-op pharmacy, other small cooperative businesses, and a community development credit union

Funding

• Catholic Charities

• State of California CETA Program

• VISTA

• Campaign for Human Development

Project/Group Structure

• 7 paid staff members

• 25 volunteers (sources of volunteers: Community Outreach persons of West Oakland, Board of Directors)

• residents of West Oakland own membership shares in the cooperative ventures

• the members of the Board of Directors of the West Oakland Food Project also sit on the Board of the West Oakland Food Cooperative

• the Project receives support from the California State Task Force on Inner City Development which is made up of experts in various economic development, community organizing, and legal fields and which is closely aligned with the state's Office of Consumer Affairs' Cooperative Development Division

Methods to Avoid/Cautions

• with outside assistance comes outside influence; since the project is of and for the West Oakland community, outside influence must be carefully monitored

Role of Religious Institutions, the Gospel, Liturgy, in Project/Group Functioning

• partial funding

III. Factsheets

FACTSHEET: The Aged

- there are 25,544,122 persons over 64 years of age in the U.S. today (out of a total population of 226,504,825)
- 15,241,532 women are over 64 (out of 116,472,530)
- 10,302,601 men are over 64 (out of 110,032,295)[1]
- in 1970 there were 291 million persons over 60 years of age in the world
- by the year 2000 there will be more than 600 million over-60s
- between 1970 and 2000 the over-60s will increase by 50% in western countries
- between 1970 and 2000 the over-60s will increase by 180% in third world countries
- by the year 2000 there will be more than 58 million persons worldwide over *80* years of age[2]
- the large proportion of those over 65 are neither seriously impaired physically nor senile[3]
- a majority of the world's elderly are poor
- more than 25% of U.S. elderly live in substandard conditions[4]

49

- old age is more difficult for women: they have earned less, therefore pensions are lower while they live longer

- approximately 1.4 million Americans retire each year[5]

- retirement means more leisure time yet less money

- a couple needs $7,198 in annual income to live at an intermediate budget level (according to the BLS)

- as of 1976 1/2 of "over 65" families had incomes below $8,721 with 1 in 7 below the poverty line of $3,417 for couples and $2,720 for individuals

- 75% of those over 65 are absent from the labor market and must rely on some kind of transfer payment for income

- social security transfers replace 1/3 to 1/2 of the average worker's pre-retirement income

- as of 1973 more than 6,000,000 retired workers received pension payments but the payments averaged less than $2,000 annually[6]

- by the year 2000 only 3 wage earners per retired person will be contributing to funding for old age pensions: this must increase 3 or 4 fold or the system will collapse[7]

- approximately half of those over 65 own or have equity in their place of residence[8]

- the number of elderly who live in single-room occupancy housing is increasing, yet the supply of such housing (chiefly in deteriorated commercial zones) is decreasing[9]

- there are over 1,250,000 elderly residents in nursing homes[10]

- in 1978 those over 65 accounted for 11% of the population but 29% of the health care costs

- although LBJ's intent was for Medicare to pay for 80% of the elderly's medical bills it only pays 38%[11]

- an estimated 3,000,000 alcoholics in the U.S. today are over-60s[12]

To Think About

- the possibility of providing home health care for the majority of the frail elderly

- since 1/2 of elderly have some equity in their places of residence, look into reverse mortgage loan programs (check with Broadview Savings, Independence, Ohio 44131, a pioneer in reverse mortgage programs for the elderly)

- holistic health programs for the elderly are meeting with success (check with Boston University's "Outlook" program)

• the idea of the "day hospital" which is a full-day program of treatment with the elderly returning home at night is perhaps an idea whose time has come (check with the Burke Rehabilitation Center, White Plains, New York)

• some gerontologists think that education programs are needed to alert the elderly to problems arising from mixing alcohol with their medications

• information on the displaced elderly, congregate housing, Section 8 subsidized housing for the elderly can be obtained by contacting HUD

• check into nursing home care in your locality and state (check state statutes for standards)

Resources

for information about home health care programs write for a transcript of "There's No Place Like Home," narrated by Helen Hayes, to: WNET, 356 W. 58th Street, New York, NY 10019

American Association of Retired Persons
1909 K Street, N.W.
Washington, D.C. 20049

Asociacion Nacional Pro Personas Mayores
(focus: hispanic elderly)
3875 Wilshire Blvd., Suite 401
Los Angeles, CA 90010

Association for Humanistic Gerontology
1711 Solano Avenue
Berkeley, CA 94707

Gray Panthers
3635 Chestnut Street
Philadelphia, PA 19104

Legal Services for the Elderly Poor
(maintains library, conducts research, litigation, and educational programs)
2095 Broadway
New York, NY 10023

National Alliance of Senior Citizens
P.O. Box 28008
Washington, D.C. 20005

National Center on Black Aged
1424 K Street, N.W., Suite 500
Washington, D.C. 20005

National Council on the Aging
1828 L Street, N.W.
Washington, D.C. 20036

National Council of Senior Citizens
1511 K Street, N.W.
Washington, D.C. 20005

Older Americans Volunteer Programs
ACTION
Washington, D.C. 20525

Self Actualization and Growth Explorations
The SAGE Project
114 Montecito Avenue
Oakland, CA 94610

Urban Elderly Coalition
1828 L Street, N.W., Suite 505
Washington, D.C. 20036

FACTSHEET:
Child Development and Youth

• in 1979, 122 million children were born worldwide; within 12 months 1 in 10 were dead—victims of disease, starvation, underdevelopment, poverty and other preventable causes[1]

• 72,444,127 persons in the U.S. are under the age of 20 years (or 32% of a total population of approximately 26.5 million.

• under 5 years of age: approximately 7.2% (16,344,407)

• ages 5-9 years: approximately 7.4% (16,697,134)

• ages 10-14 years: approximately 8.1% (18,240,919)

• ages 15-19 years: approximately 9.3% (21,161,667)[2]

• more than 1 million children in the U.S. alone are the victims of physical abuse or neglect

• 2,000 children die annually (5 or 6 daily) from circumstances associated with abuse or neglect[3]

• there are 500,000 foster children in the U.S., almost 4 times the 1961 number

• more than 50% of these children have been taken from parents with emotional or drinking problems[4]

• fewer than 10% are removed due to physical abuse[5]

• 31% of foster children had parents who simply didn't want them

• the average age of foster children is 11.7 years and rising[6]

• in New York foster care costs $10,000 per year per child

• the usual government subsidies for foster care are $25-45 per week

• less than 1/5 of New York City's 23,000 foster children find permanent homes each year (although on checking files bureaucrats found that there were numerous unanswered letters from families wishing to assist foster children)[7]

• as youth gang membership soars, the unemployment rate for white youths aged 16-19 years is 14.6%, for black and other youths aged 16-19 years it is 36.3%[8]

To Think About

• a South Carolina law that mandates a foster child's case must be reviewed every 6 months; if after 3 reviews the child has not been returned home or permanently placed, proceedings are begun to

53

terminate parental rights; prior to the law only 5.8% of the children left foster care in a year's time; now 33% are permanently placed within 6 months[9]

• temporary support services for the families of inadequately cared for children who are removed from a home might be a decisive help

• far greater numbers of children suffer emotional neglect, abuse or assault than also suffer physical abuse

• the "special needs" children in your state (children who are waiting to be adopted who are over 9 years of age, have physical or mental disabilities, are emotionally disturbed, are a member of a minority or sibling group that needs to be adopted as one): for information about such children in your state call or write the National Adoption Information Exchange (NAIE), 67 Irving Place, New York, New York 10003, 212-254-7410

Resources

"Child Abuse and Neglect: A Trainer's Manual" is available for $7.50 from the Parents' and Children's Services of the Children's Mission, 329 Longwood Avenue, Boston, Massachusetts 02115

The National Directory of Children and Youth Services: Child Protection Report is available for $42 from the NDCYS at 1301 20th Street, N.W., Washington, D.C. 20036

A report is available of the findings of the Mid-Atlantic Regional Hearings of the National Commission for Children in Need of Parents (report identifies barriers to permanent homes for foster care children, recommends action on local, state, and federal levels to correct these problems); write the Edna McConnell Clark Foundation, 250 Park Avenue, New York, New York 10017

For information about the provisions of the Federal Family Education Rights and Privacy Act, write the Dept. of Health and Human Services, 200 Independence Avenue, S.W., Washington, D.C. 20201

Write for a copy of the "Children's Agenda for Action" (which was presented as testimony by children to the Senate Subcommittee on Child and Human Development); available from Save the Children, 48 Wilton Road, Westport, Connecticut 06880

The County Office of Protective Services in Westchester County, New York, uses the Center for Preventive Psychiatry (19 Greenridge Avenue, White Plains, New York 10605) as a clinical treatment facility for children who have been abused and/or neglected; the Center also initiated a pilot project in the area of preventive intervention with young foster children at the time of their first placement

CARE
660 First Avenue
New York, New York 10016

Children's Defense Fund
(provides long range advocacy on behalf of children, drafts legislation, testifies, monitors federal agencies, engages in litigation, community organizing, works with interested groups)
1520 New Hampshire Avenue, N.W.
Washington, D.C. 20036

Child Welfare League of America
(works for improved care and services for deprived and neglected children and their families, maintains library and placement service)
67 Irving Place
New York, New York 10003

Children's Rights, Inc.
(focus: children of divorced parents and custody enforcement)
3443 17th Street, N.W.
Washington, D.C. 20010

Children's Rights Project (ACLU)
(focus: litigation, education, and public policy affecting families and children)
132 W. 43rd Street
New York, New York 10036

Children's Village, U.S.A.
(residential program for abused children and their families)
22311 Ventura Blvd.
Woodland Hills, California 91364

Division for Physically Handicapped, Dept. of Special Education
(focus: educators and those involved in supportive services to physically handicapped or health impaired children whether in or out of school, at home, or institutionalized)
University of Cincinnati
Cincinnati, Ohio 45221

Foster Parents Plan
155 Plan Way
Warwick, Rhode Island 02887

Holt International Children's Services
(provides adoption and other services to children in Korea, India, the Philippines, Thailand, Nicaragua, and the United States)
P.O. Box 2420
Eugene, Oregon 97402

Instituto Interamericano Del Nino
(part of OAS, carries out activities re child welfare and education in the

Pan American countries, maintains a large library)
Av. 8 De Octubre 2904
Montevideo, Uruguay

National Association for Child Development and Education
(represents the private child care provider in policy-making and administrative actions of the Dept. of Health and Human Services)
1800 M Street, N.W., Suite 1030N
Washington, D.C. 20036

National Center on Child Abuse and Neglect
P.O. Box 1182
Washington, D.C. 20013
202-755-0590

National Center for the Prevention and Treatment of Child Abuse and Neglect
International Society for the Prevention of Child Abuse and Neglect
(in addition to research, provides professional training for those working with abused children and their families)
University of Colorado Medical Center
1205 Oneida Street
Denver, Colorado 80220

National Child Labor Committee
(parent organization of the National Committee on Employment of Youth and the National Committee on the Education of Migrant Children)
1501 Broadway, Suite 1111
New York, New York 10036

National Committee for the Prevention of Child Abuse
332 S. Michigan Avenue, Suite 1250
Chicago, Illinois 60604

National Director of Children and Youth Services
1301 20th Street, N.W.
Washington, D.C. 20036

National Runaway Hotline: 800-621-4000
(Illinois: 800-972-6004)

National Network of Runaway and Youth Services
1705 De Sales Street, N.W., Suite 801
Washington, D.C. 20036
202-466-4212
(Ask them about the Missing Children Act of 1981, HR 3781)

The Pearl S. Buck Foundation, Inc.
(to sponsor an Amerasian boy or girl)
Green Hills Farm
Perkasie, Pennsylvania 18944

Society for Research in Child Development
(furthers interdisciplinary research in child development)
University of Chicago
5801 Ellis Avenue
Chicago, Illinois 60637

UNICEF
331 E. 38th Street
New York, New York 10016

FACTSHEET: Criminal Justice

• the criminal justice complex includes law makers, law enforcers, judicial system components (courts, public defense, prosecution, parole, probation), corrections, criminal justice information systems, research and evaluative efforts, and those who commit or who are suspected of committing crimes

• main classes of offenders: male/female/adult/juvenile

• other key categorizations: sentenced and unsentenced, first offenders and repeated offenders, felons and misdemeanants

• 30% of U.S. households touched by crime in 1980

• 6% touched by violent crime (rape, robbery, assault), 14% experienced crimes of personal larceny, 7% crimes of burglary, 10% of households experienced a household larceny, 2% a motor vehicle theft

• 38% of the crimes touched families with incomes over $25,000, 25% of the crimes touched families with incomes under $7,500

• an approximately equal proportion of crimes touched blacks and whites, urban and suburban households overall[1] (in Chicago and Oakland 70% of the homicide victims are black)[2]

• crime rate up 9% in 1980 from 1979

• a violent crime is committed every 27 seconds in this country[3]

• 1/4 of homicide victims are killed by relatives, 1/3 by strangers, the remaining by people they know[4]

• there will have been 21,000 murders in our country by the close of 1981[5]

• most offenders are not caught (there are arrests for only 1 in 5 crimes committed[6]), far fewer are prosecuted and a very small percentage are incarcerated

• there are 20 to 30 million gun *owners* in our country

• in the November 1980 election the National Rifle Association spent $1 million to support pro-gun candidates across the country[7]

• a January 1981 Gallup poll showed 38% of Americans surveyed as favoring a ban on handguns, up 7% from November 1979; 62% feel handgun laws should be made more strict, up 3% from 1979

• the "comprehensive planning" for criminal justice which was set in motion with the Omnibus Crime Control and Safe Streets Act of 1968 has not worked and has been largely dismantled

• dangerous disparities exist in definitions of crimes and in ranges of sentencing among the fifty states

-robbery in West Virginia averages 5 years longer than the average sentence for murder in 11 states

-forcible rape averages nearly 10 years in Arkansas but only 14 months in Alabama and Nevada

-auto theft in Virginia averages nearly 4 years, more than the average convicted rapist spends incarcerated in 28 states[8]

-the median time served for homicide in Massachusetts is less than 2½ years[9]

• a majority of states have reinstated the death penalty since the 1972 Supreme Court decision held that *as then imposed* the death penalty was a violation of the 8th amendment to the Constitution

• more than 700 wait on death rows

• "so far, the return of the death penalty hasn't noticeably slowed the rising homicide rate"[10]

• as of January 1, 1981, there were 292,245 adult felons sentenced to more than one year in state prisons, 21,449 in federal prisons (1979 figures: 275,850 and 24,921)

• as of January 1, 1981, 6,889 of the state figure were backed up in county jails due to overcrowded prisons[11]

• as of February 1, 1981, there were, in addition to Washington, D.C. (jails), Puerto Rico and the Virgin Islands, 36 states in which there were either existing court decrees or pending litigation dealing with overcrowding and/or total conditions of the prisons[12]

• 150 new prisons have been built in the last decade

• 41 states have 62 prisons under construction and 82 more have been proposed (as of March 1981)[13]

• each new prison cell costs an average of $60,000[14]

• it costs from $10,000 to $30,000 to keep a felon in prison for one year[15]

• at the end of 1979 196,500 men and women were on parole from correctional facilities at all levels in the U.S.

• of 64,000 people paroled in 1974-75 25% had parole revoked or returned to prison

• at the end of 1979 there were 590,772 cases under parole supervision or community supervision agencies (cases: probationers, juveniles, pre-trial diversion cases, civil drug cases, people on conditional release) with 8,303 in staff to supervise (average caseload of 71 persons)[16]

• there are more than 20 federal agencies responsible for enforcing white collar crime statutes

• white collar crime includes crimes against federal, state, or local government by public officials, crimes against the government by private citizens, crimes against business, crimes against consumers, crimes against investors, crimes against employees, crimes affecting the health and safety of the general public[17]

To Think About

• alternatives to incarceration or detention: restitution, community service sentences, greater use of probation, release on recognizance, increased use of summons instead of arrest, system of fines allowing installment payments, more equitable bail system

• no new construction of jails or prisons

• setting minimum standards for existing jails and prisons

• promoting community-based corrections

• monitoring your criminal (and civil) courts[18]

• providing social workers in police departments

• promoting victim/witness programs in police departments as well as in State's Attorneys' offices along with guidelines and operating procedures

• promoting the idea of a more uniform crime code

• enabling prosecutors to zero in on major (repeat) offenders

• becoming familiar with your state's criminal code

• monitoring your state legislature in the area of criminal justice especially its House and Senate Judiciary committees

• "At current levels . . . a typical baby born and remaining in a large American city is more likely to die of murder than an American soldier in World War II was to die in combat."[19]

• should criminal law be used to enforce private morality and business ethics?[20]

Resources

for the interim and final report of the 1981 Attorney General's Task Force on Violent Crime, write the U.S. Department of Justice, Office of Public Affairs, Washington, D.C. 20530

for a copy of the Kennedy-Rodino Handgun Crime Control Act of 1981 bill, contact one or the other of their offices (S 974 & H.R. 3200)

an old and good victim/witness assistance program is operating in California: contact Sterling O'Ran, Director, Office of Criminal Justice Planning, 9719 Lincoln Valley Drive, Suite 600, Sacramento, CA 95827

Americans for Human Rights and Social Justice
(focus: elderly, disabled and socially disadvantaged in the corrections system)
109 Bent Bridge Road
Greenville, South Carolina 29611

Crime Prevention Coalition
Box 6600
Rockville, Maryland 20850

Fund for Modern Courts
36 West 44th Street, Room 711
New York, New York 10036

Handgun Control, Inc.
810 18th Street, N.W.
Washington, D.C. 20006

Hartford Institute of Criminal and Social Justice
15 Lewis Street, Suite 501
Hartford, Connecticut 06103

International Halfway House Association
2525 Victory Parkway, Suite 101
Cincinnati, Ohio 45206

John Howard Association
(focus: prison reform and prevention and
control of crime and delinquency)
67 E. Madison
Chicago, Illinois 60603

National Alliance of Handgun Control Organizations
P.O. Box 15371
Nashville, Tennessee 37215

National Association of Criminal Justice Planners
1012 14th Street, N.W., Suite 403
Washington, D.C. 20005

National Association of State Directors of
Law Enforcement Training
c/o Massachusetts Criminal Justice Training Council
1 Ashburton Place
Boston, Massachusetts 02108

National Bureau of Justice Statistics
Washington, D.C. 20531

National Coalition Against the Death Penalty
132 W. 43rd Street
New York, New York 10036

National Council on Crime and Delinquency
(maintains a library)
411 Hackensack Avenue
Hackensack, New Jersey 07601

National Criminal Justice Reference Service
Box 6000
Rockville, Maryland 20850

National Institute of Justice
633 Indiana Avenue, N.W.
Washington, D.C. 20531

National Institute for Sentencing Alternatives
Ford Hall, 2nd Floor
Brandeis University
Waltham, Massachusetts 02254
(ask this office about the new
sentencing guidelines in Minnesota)

National Moratorium on Prison Construction
324 C Street, S.E.
Washington, D.C. 20003

National Organization for Victim Assistance
8565 S.W. Salish Lane
Wilsonville, Oregon 97070

National Prison Project (ACLU)
1346 Connecticut Avenue, N.W., Suite 1031
Washington, D.C. 20036

Vera Institute of Justice
(conducts research/action projects in criminal justice reform and in
helping those considered unemployable into the job market)
30 E. 39th Street
New York, New York 10016

FACTSHEET:
Drugs and Addiction

- 4 basic categories of drugs
  depressants:
  e.g., narcotics, barbiturates, hypno-sedatives, tranquilizers, alcohol
  stimulants:
  e.g., cocaine, dexedrine, diet pills, caffeine, nicotine
  hallucinogens:
  e.g., LSD, STP, DMT, marijuana
  inhalants:
  e.g., vaporized chemicals such as glue, paint thinner, gasoline

- drugs most commonly enter the body by capsule or tablet, liquid, injectibile solutions, intravenous or intramuscular, suppository, vapor by inhalation[1]

- many drugs are physiologically addictive (heroin, alcohol)

- other drugs are psychologically addictive (cocaine, marijuana)

- 100,000 to 300,000 persons in this country are addicted to heroin[2] (many more use the drug but are in earlier stages of dependency)

- approximately 10,000,000 persons abuse alcohol in the U.S.

- 1 in 4 persons drinks too much

- 1 in 8 persons reports liquor as a source of trouble in his or her family[3]

- of the 50,000 persons killed in traffic accidents yearly in our country, 50% of the accidents involve substantial blood alcohol levels in either the driver or the victim[4]

- the barbiturates secobarbital (Seconal) and pentobarbital (Luminal) are the most commonly abused drugs after alcohol and tobacco[5] (and caffeine)

- caffeine is a drug of the xanthine group which is found in coffee, tea, cocoa, and many soft drinks

- 25% of Americans over age 17 drink 6 or more cups of tea or coffee per day[6]

- in 1968 the Bureau of Narcotics and the Bureau of Drug Abuse Control were combined to form the Bureau of Narcotics and Dangerous Drugs (Department of Justice) which has federal level responsibility for the entire drug problem

- *"Comprehensive Drug Abuse Prevention and Control Act of 1970*: Replaced previous acts (more than 50 different laws previously enacted) for control of narcotics, marijuana, sedatives, and stimulants and placed their control under the Department of Justice. Drugs are classified into five schedules according to their potential for abuse and therapeutic usefulness. First-time illegitimate possession of any drug in the five schedules is considered a misdemeanor and penalties are reduced. Provisions are made for rehabilitation, education, and research. House search ("no-knock" law) was legalized."

- Schedule I: substances with no recognized medical use but a high potential for abuse (e.g., heroin, marijuana, peyote, mescaline, LSD, DET, DMT, THC)
- Schedule II: substances with some medical use but a high potential for abuse (e.g., codeine, opium, morphine, Dilaudid, Methadone, Demerol, cocaine)
- Schedule III: substances used medically with a moderate to high potential for abuse (e.g., paregoric, Empirin with codeine, ASA with codeine, Doriden, Preludin, Ritalin)
- Schedule IV: substances used in medicine with low potential for abuse (e.g., phenobarbital, chloral hydrate, paraldehyde, Equanil, Miltown) (Valium and Librium have been or are about to be moved up from this category.)
- Schedule V: substances formerly known as "exempt narcotics" (e.g., cough syrups containing codeine)[7]

• *"Drug Abuse Office and Treatment Act*: (1972) Brought about by the increasing drug use by U.S. troops in Vietnam and increased use in the United States, this law established the Special Action Office for Drug Abuse Prevention to be the coordinator of the nine federal agencies involved in drug abuse activities. With an emphasis on treatment and rehabilitation programs, SAODAP develops federal strategies for all drug abuse efforts other than drug traffic prevention. Also detailed in the legislation was the establishment of the National Institute on Drug Abuse, which took place in April 1974. This organization will continue the programs established by SAODAP."[8]

To Think About

• supporting any public policy or legislation which focuses on *treatment* of drug abusers

• "It appears to be easier to make laws than to change them. The Marijuana Tax Act (1937) and Uniform Narcotic Drug Act (1932) are both quite old, and one must consider the information that was available when the lawmakers formed their opinions concerning marijuana."[9]

• Maine's new drinking and driving law which makes driving with a blood-alcohol content of 10% *a crime in itself*

- a lethal dose of caffeine could be consumed in drinking 20 cups of coffee all at once[10]

- purging the words "reformed addict" and "reformed alcoholic" from your vocabulary, using instead "recovered addict" or "recovered alcoholic"

Resources

Domestic Council Drug Abuse Task Force, *White Paper on Drug Abuse*, U.S. Govt. Printing Office, Washington, D.C., 1975

Report of the National Commission on the Causes and Prevention of Violence, "The Problem of Over-Criminalization," in *Law and Order Reconsidered*, pp. 551-567, U.S. Govt. Printing Office, Washington, D.C., 1969

For guidelines on requesting monetary support for your activities write The Bureau of Narcotics and Dangerous Drugs, Prevention Programs Division, 1405 Eye St., N.W., Washington, D.C. 20537

Regional offices of the Bureau of Narcotics and Dangerous Drugs will loan certain films free to civic organizations

Alcoholics Anonymous World Services
P.O. Box 459
Grand Central Station
New York, New York 10017

Al-Anon Family Group Headquarters
One Park Avenue
New York, New York 10016

American Council on marijuana and Other Psychoactive Drugs
(resource information kits including written and audio-visual materials)
767 Fifth Avenue
New York, New York 10022

Association of Halfway House Alcoholic Programs of N. America
(educates and serves halfway house programs)
786 E. Seventh Street
St. Paul, Minnesota 55106

National Association on Drug Abuse Problems
(sponsored by business and labor; focus is on rehabilitation, employment and prevention programs)
355 Lexington Avenue
New York, New York 10017

National Association of State Alcohol and Drug Abuse Directors
(represents state directors to the federal government and Congress)
1612 K Street, N.W., Suite 900
Washington, D.C. 20006

National Clearinghouse for Alcohol Information
National Institute on Alcoholic Abuse and Alcoholism
Box 2345
Rockville, Maryland 20852

National Clearinghouse for Drug Abuse Information
5454 Wisconsin Avenue
Chevy Chase, Maryland 20015

National Council on Alcoholism
(maintains library; focus is on prevention and control through education, community services, promotion of alcoholism research)
733 Third Avenue
New York, New York 10017

National Council on Drug Abuse
(conducts research and disseminates information)
571 W. Jackson
Chicago, Illinois 60606

Odyssey Institute
(focus: drug treatment and special projects include therapist training, operates residential treatment communities in 5 states)
656 Avenue of the Americas
New York, New York 10010

Women for Sobriety
(focus: alcoholic women)
P.O. Box 618
Quakertown, Pennsylvania 18951

FACTSHEET:
Economic Development

- 11.4% of the total U.S. population in 1978 or 24,497,000 persons were poor

- 8.7% (16,259,000) of the white population are poor

- 30.6% (7,625,000) of the black population are poor

- 5.9% of male-head families are poor (9,793,000)

- 35.6% of female-head families are poor (9,269,000)

- 51% of all black female heads of families are poor (1,208,000)[1]

- more than 9,000,000 central city residents were poor in 1978[2] (15% of Buffalo residents and 26% of New Orleans residents)[3]

- although blacks make up about 23% of the nation's central city populations, they make up 48% of the central city poor

- while white central city poor declined by 14% between 1969 and 1978, black central city poor rose by 19%[4]

- 112 cities lost population between 1960 and 1970; 180 cities lost population between 1970 and 1979

- declining population in cities is most severe in the Middle Atlantic region, where three out of four cities are losing population[5] (the better-off departing, the poor remaining)

- three major federal policies have encouraged regional decentralization
    "-*defense*: defense payrolls have been concentrated in the South, defense contracts in the West
    -*public works*: inland waterway projects have opened up land-locked southern cities to profitable international markets; highways, subsidized by northern taxes, have allowed the economic integration of the South
    -*tax structure*: the tax structure has favored new investment in growth areas at the expense of maintenance and repair investment in older cities"[6]

- four federal policies have directly encouraged businesses to suburbanize
    "-*tax structure*: new investments have been subsidized, as have capital intensive plants that require large lots
    -*freight rate regulation*: regulation has contributed to the deterioration of rail to the benefit of trucking
    -*infrastructure grants*: federal grants have facilitated suburban expansion

- *-highways*: highways have allowed firms and workers to move away from rail spurs and mass transit routes"[7]

- three federal policies "have contributed to the selective suburbanization of middle income households, leaving the cities populated with low income minorities
    - *-homeownership subsidies*: tax advantages and mortgage subsidies have led households to move to new housing in the suburbs, where construction has been subsidized by federal infrastructure grants and tax policies
    - *-housing for the poor*: programs have located most public housing in central cities
    - *-social services*: together with low income housing, the greater accessibility of social services for the disadvantaged in central cities has discouraged the out-migration of the poor"[8]

- urban economic development problems include: unemployment and poverty (possibly arising from lack of training or work experience), poor local business climate (due to obsolete infrastructure, land fragmentation, poor access, vandalism, etc.), local jurisdiction's fiscal inability to provide good services, political fragmentation in metro areas, changes in the patterns of international trade or federal purchases, severe economic dislocation (floods or a military base closing, for example), air and water pollution, inadequate information flow (for example, in the labor market), inequitable pricing (as in the case of labor wages)[9]

- areas of existing or possible government assistance in economic development include: tax incentives, wage subsidies, business loans, training programs, revenue sharing, community development block grants, public works programs, sewer and water treatment grants, mass transit assistance[10]

To Think About

- "Available evidence suggests that federal tax, housing, and regulatory policies may have a greater effect on urban economic development than direct federal assistance programs."[11]

- capturing and channeling pension funds to help reinvigorate the economy of states (pension funds are now worth $650 billion in assets and by 1995 are likely to reach $4 trillion)[12]

- "Economic development consists in enlarging the opportunity for those so motivated to escape the . . . culture of poverty."[13]

- "It is by universal education—literacy and its employment—that individuals gain access to the world outside the culture of poverty and its controlling equilibrium."[14]

Resources

For information about pension funds for use as social investment write to the Governor's office in Sacramento, California, for the public-investment task force report

The Nature of Mass Poverty, John Kenneth Galbraith, Harvard University Press: Cambridge, Massachusetts, 1979

"This Land is Home to Me," Pastoral of the Catholic Bishops of Appalachia, contained in *Flesh and Spirit: a Religious View of Bicentennial America*, Community for Creative Nonviolence, Washington, D.C. 1976 (order from Gamaliel, 1335 N Street, N.W., Washington, D.C. 20005)

Appalachian Regional Commission (U.S.)
1666 Connecticut Avenue, N.W.
Washington, D.C. 20235.

Center for Community Change
(focus: antipoverty; assists community groups of poor; designs and delivers technical assistance to community organizations)
1000 Wisconsin Avenue, N.W.
Washington, D.C. 20007
202-338-6310

Corporation for Enterprise Development
2420 K Street, N.W.
Washington, D.C. 20037
202-298-8771

Department of Health and Human Services
200 Independence Avenue, S.W.
Washington, D.C. 20201

Department of Housing and Urban Development
451 7th Street, S.W.
Washington, D.C. 20410

Department of Labor
200 Constitution Avenue, N.W.
Washington, D.C. 20210

Economic Development Administration
Department of Commerce
14th Street between Constitution and E Street, N.W.;
Washington, D.C. 20230

Economic Development Assistance Center
Opportunities Industrialization Centers of America
100 W. Coulter Street
Philadelphia, Pennsylvania 19144

Equal Employment Opportunity Commission
2401 E Street, N.W.
Washington, D.C. 20506

Local Initiatives Support Corporation (LISC)
(the Ford Foundation and 6 major private insurance, industrial and banking firms; focus: to provide a select number of community-based organizations with technical assistance and a small amount of funding—no more than $50,000/2 years matched dollar-for-dollar by local corporations' support—to increase their ability to draw upon private and public resources for neighborhood revitalization)
666 3rd Avenue
New York, New York 10017
212-949-8571

Small Business Administration
1441 L Street, N.W.
Washington, D.C. 20416

FACTSHEET: Education

- 1978 5-17 year old population: 48,015,000[1]

- 1978 public school enrollment, elementary and high school: 42,559,000; (elementary—25,030,000; high school—17,529,000 with 2.5-3 million graduating from high school each year)[2]

- in 1978 approximately 6,000,000 children were enrolled in private schools, were in other institutions or were not in school

- in public schools in 1978 there were 2,199,000 classroom teachers

- in 1978 there were 15,992 local school systems in the U.S.[3]

- the average school term is 178.3 days per year[4]

- estimated total expenditures for public elementary and secondary schools in 1977 was $81,097,000

- 1977 average salary of classroom teacher: $14,244

- 1976-77 average cost per pupil varied widely by state: on the high end are Alaska ($3,890), New York ($2,645), the District of Columbia ($2,467), New Jersey ($2,285), Massachusetts ($2,230); on the low end are Arkansas ($1,218), Mississippi ($1,225), Kentucky ($1,233), Alabama ($1,327), Tennessee ($1,334)[5]

- federal funds for education (1979—excluding loans, school lunch programs, etc.): elementary and secondary—$6½ billion, higher education—$9 billion, vocational education—$6 billion[6]

To Think About

- what of an educational nature is happening to children the other 186.7 days per year?

- "the schools must serve as the principal medium for developing in youth the attitudes and skills of social, political, and cultural criticism . . . a continuing struggle against the veneration of 'crap' "[7]

- "the purpose of the 'new education' is to produce people who can cope effectively with (rapid) change"[8]

- "develop skills, attitudes, habits of mind and the kinds of knowledge and understanding that will be the instruments of continuous change and growth on the part of the young person . . . then we will have fashioned *a system that provides for its own continuous renewal*"[9]

- we need to educate keeping in mind that the mind is an instrument to be used rather than a storehouse to be filled[10]

- "the art and science of asking questions is the source of all knowledge . . . question asking . . . has to deal with problems that are perceived as useful and realistic by the learners"[11]

- "the intellectual virtues are the proximate ends of all truly *liberal* or *intellectual* education . . . four virtues . . . the arts . . . understanding, science and wisdom . . . wisdom is the highest end and the controlling principle in any consideration of the means"[12]

- "The test of a school or of an educational philosophy is how well it educates *all* kinds of children—rich, poor, smart, stupid, black, white."[13]

Resources

The Changing Classroom, Carol Goodell (ed.), Ballantine Books: New York, 1973.

Crisis in the Classroom: The Remaking of American Education, Charles E. Silberman, Random House: New York, 1970.

Reforming Education, Mortimer Adler, Westview Press: Boulder, Colorado, 1977.

The School Book, Neil Postman and Charles Weingartner, Delacorte Press: New York, 1973.

Teaching as a Subversive Activity, Neil Postman and Charles Weingartner, Dell: New York, 1969.

Values Clarification, S.B. Simon, L.W. Howe and H. Kirschenbaum, Hart: New York, 1972.

Center for Educational Reform
P.O. Box 10085
Eugene, Oregon 97401

Institute of Wholistic Education
Box 575
Amherst, Massachusetts 01002

National Education Association
1201 16th Street, N.W.
Washington, D.C. 20036

National Foundation for the Improvement of Education
(parent organization is NEA)
1201 16th Street, N.W., Room 804E
Washington, D.C. 20036

Parent Teacher Association, National (PTA)
700 N. Rush Street
Chicago, IL 60611

U.S. Department of Education
Washington, D.C. 20202
(just to be sure, mark envelope "Please Forward If Necessary"

Your state office of education

Your local school district office

FACTSHEET: The Environment

- the relatively thin layer of air which stretches from the surface of the earth toward outer space is some 5 to 11 miles deep[1]

- an estimated 125-150 million tons of aerial garbage are dumped each year[2]

- 35 million tons of hazardous waste are produced each year[3] (all fired up with no place to go)

- "acid rain" is killing the fish in the Adirondack lakes and is estimated will "kill" tens of thousands of Canadian lakes (half of Canada's acid rain originates in the U.S.)[4]

- everything from PCBs to highway salt is tainting our drinking water

- much of the 1.3 billion pounds of pesticides produced in the world each year ends up in the oceans[5]

- oceans, the final dumping ground for all pollution, cover 71% of the earth and are remarkably shallow for their size

- less than half of 1% of the ocean space represents the home of *90%* of all marine life (these are the coastal waters, the dumping grounds for sewage and silt from chemically treated farmland)[6]

- all water comes as rain from the sky, but 92% of it runs off unused into the oceans or evaporates

- we in the U.S. use 21 billion gallons *more* of water per day than we receive from rain

- 25% of the water which irrigates, powers and is used in our homes comes from a network of ancient underground aquifers (61 billion gallons/day seep into the aquifers from rain; we withdraw *82* billion gallons per day)[7]

- of the total 106 billion gallons of water which we use per day,
  - 6.9% is for domestic use
  - 1.3% goes to power generation
  - 1.3% goes to public lands
  - 7.7% goes to manufacturing and mining
  - 82.7% goes to agriculture[8]

- it takes 14,935 gallons of water to grow one bushel of wheat, 120 gallons to produce a single egg

- the water that goes into a 1,000 lb. steer would float a destroyer (a single steak may have accounted for 3,500 gallons of water—beginning with the water that irrigated the corn that fed the steer)

- it takes 60,000 gallons of water to produce one ton of steel[9] ("despite the recycling of steel, the manufacture of new cars still accounts for 10% of *all* industrial energy use")[10]

- Energy: THE SUN
  - solar energy now supplies 6% of our total energy needs (chiefly in the form of hydroelectric power and wood)
  - solar could meet more than the official goal of 20% of our energy needs by the year 2000
  - each year the sun drenches the earth in 500 times more energy than we consume[11]

- Energy: WIND
  - it would take 30,000 large turbines and thousands of smaller ones to supply 10% of the nation's electric power by the year 2000
  - the Wind Energy Systems Act of 1980 initiated an eight year, $900 million program to develop cost effective wind-power systems in this country
  - a number of large wind turbines are in the experimental testing or development stages[12]

- Energy: GEOTHERMAL
  - it is estimated that by the year 2020 geothermal energy could supply 17% of the nation's energy needs
  - 2,300,000 acres of federal land have been leased for exploration and development of this "earth heat"
  - hot springs have heated homes in Boise, Idaho, since the late 19th century
  - dry steam with high pressure and low water content drives turbines at The Geysers in California, producing electricity equal to half of San Francisco's consumption[13]

- Energy: NATURAL GAS
  - gas supplies 26% of our current energy needs
  - although drilling for both oil and natural gas reached an all-time high in 1980, only 25% of the drilling effort was devoted to gas
  - although most analysts predict little change in gas supplies in the U.S. in the foreseeable future, policymakers are advocating turning to imports of natural gas from Canada, Mexico and shipment of liquefied natural gas (LNG) from Arab states and Indonesia, constructing a gas pipeline from Alaska, and engaging in the costly process of coal gasification[14]

- Energy: COAL
  - coal provides 20% of our energy each year
  - of the 680 million tons of coal consumed in the U.S in 1979, 77% was used by electric utilities
  - in 1979 250,000 U.S. miners worked in 6,000 mines in 26 states producing 780 million tons of coal
  - at present levels of use, world coal reserves (concentrated in the U.S., U.S.S.R., and China) would last the world more than 200 years, estimating conservatively
  - the U.S. has the largest portion, 25% of the world's 789 billion tons of coal reserves

- geologists think the world probably has 15 times this amount
- in addition the U.S. has 1.7 trillion tons of coal deposits at depths of less than 3,000 feet (inaccessible for the most part with present technology and prices)
- environmental considerations of further coal mining include climate changes due to increased carbon dioxide, emissions from coal stacks that erode buildings, poison lakes and damage lungs, proper reclamation of mine sites[15]

- Energy: OIL
  - domestic and imported oil combine to provide 45% of our current energy needs
  - in 1980 Americans consumed each day more than 25% of the 60 million barrels of oil produced worldwide
  - 9 million barrels per day come from domestic wells (U.S. is third after the U.S.S.R. and Saudi Arabia, among world producers)
  - 7 million barrels a day must be imported from OPEC countries (whose 13 member nations produce half of the world's oil)
  - at current production levels, the U.S. has nine years of domestic oil reserves left[16]

- Energy: URANIUM
  - 72 nuclear power plants in operation in the U.S. provide 3.7% of our total energy needs, 10% of our electricity
  - 85 plants are under construction, 19 more are on order (as of February 1981)
  - a pound of uranium enriched fuel contains almost 3 million times the energy in a pound of coal
  - almost ½ of the world's uranium lies in the western U.S.
  - new orders for nuclear power plants have declined due to higher construction costs, reduced electrical demand through conservation, tighter regulations and increasing public opposition
  - the radioactive power produced requires extreme precautions in plant operation and construction and in "disposing" of nuclear waste materials[17]
  - reactor operators are running out of pool space in which to store the highly radioactive wastes such as spent fuel rods

To Think About

- "It cannot be stressed enough that we should take into account the larger ecosystem in treating a seemingly local (environmental) problem"[18]

- conservationists argue that if we err in favor of conservation, at least choices will remain open to us in the future[19]

- "The worldwide fish catch started down in 1971, and it hasn't stopped sliding yet. Better equipment. Better vessels. And worse catches."[20]

- "Solutions to the major problems of our time—energy, food, minerals, population—can be found only if we do not slight the vital importance of a healthy global water system rooted in the ocean. As far as energy is concerned, the only source that may create irreversible conditions threatening our survival is atomic energy: logically, it should be banned worldwide. At the opposite pole, the only inexhaustible and totally harmless source of energy is the sun. Direct solar heating and cooling, conversion of light into electricity, modern wind-powered generators, ocean thermal-energy conversion plants, currents, waves, open-ocean kelp farms . . . an all-out worldwide effort could bring about, by the turn of the century, global self-sufficiency with hydrogen and methane replacing gasoline and natural gas. To bridge the twenty-five year gap, oil, offshore oil, and coal could be exploited with acceptable standards of safety for our environment. The vast investments needed for such a policy can be found only if our costly nuclear mistakes are stopped immediately; the transition would be greatly helped by energy-conservation measures. Such a plan will inevitably be adopted someday, but the sooner the switch, the smaller the cost . . . and the risk."[21]

- the "Kemeny Report" (the report of the President's Commission on the Accident at Three-Mile Island) called for over 40 changes regarding nuclear power generation and its regulation, including:
  - the abolishment of the 5-member Nuclear Regulatory Commission and the forming of an agency with a single director named by the President
  - upgrading of training and qualifications for reactor operators
  - tightening of federal licensing procedures and periodic review of licenses (presently utilities are licensed to operate nuclear plants for the plants' expected lifetimes of 40 years with no review at all)
  - tightening of safety standards for nuclear facilities near populous areas[22]

Resources

"Are We Running Out of Water?" *Newsweek*, February 23, 1981, pp. 26-37

"Energy: A Special Report in the Public Interest," *National Geographic*, February 1981

"The Spreading Desert," Erik Eckholm and Lester R. Brown, an article available from the Worldwatch Institute, 1776 Massachusetts Avenue, N.W., Washington, D.C.

Contact the state capitol in Salem, Oregon, for a copy of Oregon's statute banning the manufacture and sale of aluminum cans and other disposable beverage containers (for information about *recycling* aluminum, write Alcoa, Dept. 507-Q, Aloca Building, Pittsburgh, PA 15219)

Alliance to Save Energy
(an alliance of corporations, small businesses, associations, unions, and individuals; focus: a clearinghouse for energy conserving facts and

information; maintains library re energy conservation and alternative sources of energy) 1925 K Street, N.W., No. 507, Washington, D.C. 20006 202-857-0666

Clergy and Laity Concerned
198 Broadway
New York, New York 10038

The Cousteau Society
Box 1881
New York, New York 10017

Department of Energy
1000 Independence Avenue, S.W.
Washington, D.C. 20585
(just to be sure, mark envelope "Please Forward If Necessary)

Department of Interior
C Street between 18th & 19th Sts., N.W.
Washington, D.C. 20240

Environmental Action
(national political lobby organization with ties to 5,000 local, state, and campus ecology groups; focus: solid waste, anti-nuclear, toxic substances, drinking water, beverage container deposit legislation, workplace and urban environment issues, lobbying, demonstrations, educational and legal action, coordinated efforts on the Clean Air Act, the Clean Water Act, Occupational Safety and Health Act, Toxic Substance Control Act and the Resource Conservation and Recovery Act in Congress)
1346 Connecticut Avenue, N.W., Suite 731
Washington, D.C. 20036

Environmental Defense Fund
162 Old Town Road
East Setauket, New York 11733
516-751-5191

(serves universities, government, others; focus: facilitating access to environmental and energy information by locating it, abstracting it, and storing it in a computerized data bank from which it may be retrieved for immediate use)

Environmental Information Center
292 Madison Avenue
New York, New York 10017

Environmental Protection Agency (EPA)
Public Information Center
401 M Street, S.W.
Washington, D.C. 20460
202-755-0707

Friends of the Earth
124 Spear Street
San Francisco, California 94105

National Solar Heating and Cooling Information Center
P.O. Box 1607
Rockville, Maryland 20850

Natural Resources Defense Council
122 East 42nd Street
New York, New York 10164

Nuclear Regulatory Commission (U.S.)
Office of Public Affairs
Washington, D.C. 20555
202-492-7715

Sierra Club
530 Bush Street
San Francisco, California 94108

Solar Energy Institute of America
(serves as center for the collection and dissemination of solar information; offers public telephone information line on all areas of solar energy and professional service)
1110 Sixth Street, N.W.
Washington, D.C. 20001
202-667-6611

Union of Concerned Scientists
1384 Massachusetts Avenue
Cambridge, Massachusetts 02238

The Wilderness Society
1901 Pennsylvania Avenue, N.W.
Washington, D.C. 20006

World Wildlife Fund-U.S.
1601 Connecticut Avenue, N.W.
Washington, D.C. 20009
202-387-0800

FACTSHEET: The Handicapped

- over 50 million Americans have physical, mental, or emotional handicaps
- 11.7 million are physically disabled
- 12.5 million are temporarily injured
- 2.4 million are deaf
- 11 million have impaired hearing
- 1.3 million are blind
- 8.2 million are visually handicapped
- 6.8 million are mentally disabled
- 1.7 million are homebound (with chronic health disorders, wasting diseases)
- 2.1 million are institutionalized (mentally disturbed, mentally retarded, terminally ill)[1]
- approximately 12 million physically and mentally handicapped Americans are of working age
- only 60% of the handicapped males of working age are employed (compared with 95% of all men of working age who are employed)
- only 29% of the handicapped females of working age are employed (compared with 54% of all females of working age who are employed)[2]
- most handicapped workers require no special work arrangement or adjustment
- there is no increase in compensation costs or lost time injuries with a handicapped worker
- 96% of handicapped workers rated average or better in safety both on and off the job
- 91% of handicapped workers are rated average or better in job performance
- 79% of handicapped workers are rated average or better in attendance[3]
- of the 2.9 million Americans who served in Indochina, nearly 100,000 returned with severe physical disabilities
- another 50,000 Vietnam veterans may have got cancer from Agent Orange
- perhaps 25% of those who served may still be subject to *substantial* psychological problems[4]

• the Veterans' Administration is a $23 billion/year agency devoted mainly to World War II veterans

• 91 federally funded counseling centers across the country have helped more than 67,000 Vietnam veterans since 1979 (in 1981 the U.S. Congress extended the program—against the wishes of the President—for three additional years, the House vote being 388 to 0)[5]

• Section 504 of the 1973 Rehabilitation Act imposed non-discrimination and affirmative action on all HEW (HHS) recipients

• another significant piece of federal legislation is the Architectural Barriers Act of 1968 and its subsequent amendments

• the 1976 Tax Reform Act provides tax deductions of up to $25,000 for companies that remodel to accommodate the needs of handicapped persons[6]

To Think About
• establishing a halfway house in your community for patients released from mental health facilities

• further extending health insurance coverage so that it routinely covers mental illness

• the institutionalized handicapped have the right to be treated with basic dignity and respect, the right to decide what is going to happen and why (including the right to consent to or refuse any treatment), the right to physical privacy and confidentiality of information, and the right to the *whole truth*, including access to medical records[7]

• hiring the handicapped

Resources
Federal Assistance for Programs Serving the Handicapped (1980) U.S. Department of Education, Office of Special Education and Rehabilitative Services, Office for Handicapped Individuals (available from the Superintendent of Documents, U.S. Govt. Printing Office, Washington, D.C. 20402)

The Law and Disabled People: Selected Federal and State Laws Affecting Employment and Certain Rights of People With Disabilities (1980) (also available from the Superintendent of Documents)

Final Summary Report, The White House Conference on Handicapped Individuals (Superintendent of Documents)

Educational Handicap, Public Policy, and Social History: A Broadened Perspective on Mental Retardation, S.B. Sarason and J. Doris, The Free Press: New York, 1979

The Hidden Minority: America's Handicapped, Sonny Kleinfield, Little Brown: Boston and Toronto, 1979

Personal Relationships, the Handicapped and the Community: Some European Thoughts and Solutions, D. Lancaster-Gaye (ed.), Routledge and Kegan Paul: London and Boston, 1972

American Association for the Advancement of Sciences, Project on the Handicapped
1515 Massachusetts Avenue, N.W.
Washington, D.C. 20005

American Coalition of Citizens with Disabilities
1346 Connecticut Avenue, N.W., Room 308
Washington, D.C. 20046
(has state and regional chapters)

(Architectural barriers)
Director, Architectural Transportation Barriers
Compliance Board
330 C Street, S.W.
Washington, D.C. 20201
202-245-1591

Chief, Clearinghouse on the Handicapped Office
Department of Health and Human Services
Washington, D.C. 20201
202-245-1961

Committee for the Handicapped/People to People Program
La Salle Building, Suite 610
Connecticut Avenue and L Street
Washington, D.C. 20036
(ask about the *Directory of Organizations Interested in the Handicapped*, 1976)

National Association for Retarded Citizens
(information on jobs for mentally retarded persons)
2709 Avenue E East
Arlington, Texas 76011

National Center for Law and the Handicapped
1235 North Eddy Street
South Bend, Indiana 46617

National Congress of Organizations
of the Physically Handicapped
7611 Oakland Avenue
Minneapolis, Minnesota 55423

(Reading material for the blind and the physically handicapped)
Director, National Library Service for the Blind
and Physically Handicapped
1291 Taylor Street, N.W.
Washington, D.C. 20542
202-882-5500

President's Committee on Employment of the Handicapped
Washington, D.C. 20210

Veterans Administration
810 Vermont Avenue, N.W.
Washington, D.C. 20420

Vietnam Veterans Against the War
(focus: testing and treatment of Agent Orange poisoning, improving conditions for veterans—job opportunities, extension and expansion of GI Bill, counseling, discharge upgrading—works against draft or registration)
P.O. Box 20184
Chicago, Illinois 60620

Vietnam Veterans of America
(focus: employment, educational benefits, improved psychological assistance and health care for Vietnam veterans)
P.O. Box 2983
Washington, D.C. 20013

FACTSHEET: Housing

- 1970 Census figures show 68.6 million housing units in the U.S. (advance 1980 Census reports show 80,376,609 households)

- as of 1970, 9.1 million households, or 1 out of 7 families, lived in substandard housing conditions[1]

- principal housing problems today are affordability and limited new construction (as of October 1981, the average yearly housing starts for 1981 was 918,000 units—that figure has only been lower twice in 20 years and has been on the average substantially higher)[2]

- disinvestment in maintenance of existing rental units, condominium conversion and abandonment of unprofitable rental housing has caused a dearth of decent units in cities (especially units of family size)

- in 1977, 50% of central city renters spent over 25% of their income on housing; 33% spent over 35%[3]

- as of 1978 the objectives of federal housing policy were:
  - ensuring the availability of adequate and affordable housing
  - increasing residential construction and reducing instability in the homebuilding industry
  - expanding access to credit
  - encouraging homeownership
  - providing equal housing opportunities
  - providing housing for special users
  - encouraging community development and neighborhood preservation and revitalization

- as of 1978 the principal federal housing programs included: (some of the programs listed may be on the way out)
  - low-rent public housing
  - Section 8 New Construction/Substantial Rehabilitation
  - Section 8 Existing Housing
  - Section 235 Homeownership Assistance
  - Section 236 Rental Assistance and Rent Supplements
  - Section 202 Housing for Elderly and Handicapped

- as of 1978 the housing-related federal programs included:
  - Community Development Block Grants
  - Urban Development Action Grants
  - Section 312 Rehabilitation Loans
  - Urban Homesteading

- as of 1978 the federal government's mortgage credit activities included
  - direct loan programs
  - mortgage insurance programs
  - credit-market interventions

- as of 1978 the federal government's housing-related tax expenditure efforts included
    - homeownership incentives
    - promoting rental housing development
    - tax benefits for financial institutions
- as of 1978 the federal government's housing and credit market regulations were directed toward
    - guaranteeing equal housing opportunities
    - controlling supply and cost of mortgage credit[4]
- tools available to states and localities to meet the housing challenge include public/private planning to make maximum use of federal assistance, effective use of revenue bonds, mortgage guarantees, mortgage insurance, direct (low interest) loans, tax incentives, zoning techniques, special procedures to quit titles, and safeguards against the abuse of incentives[5]
- the basic *regional factors* affecting a change *downward* in the quality of life in a neighborhood are:
    - population decline
    - declining job opportunities
    - new housing production
    - rising personal income
- the basic factors *internal to the neighborhood* which affect a change *downward* in the quality of neighborhood life are:
    - poor land use
    - racism
    - classism
    - redlining and racial steering
    - aging housing stock
- the basic *regional factors* affecting a change *upward* in the quality of life in a neighborhood are:
    - increasing population
    - increasing jobs
    - rising new housing production costs
    - declining real income
- the basic factors *internal to the neighborhood* which affect a change *upward* in the quality of neighborhood life are:
    - adequate maintenance investment
    - changing social attitudes
    - good land use
    - improved housing management[6]

To Think About
- approaches to meeting housing challenges must begin with an urban perspective because, as one social scientist has put it, our society is tri-level: federal, state, and urban

• the three basic components of urban life are housing, population, and jobs; housing improvement must be coordinated with over-all economic development efforts (in 1919 Edith Elmer Wood wrote in *The Housing of the Unskilled Wage Earner* that poor housing is the result of the malfunctioning of the modern industrial system and needs a much different approach from the traditionally regulatory one)

• "One approach involving all levels of government, citizens and the private sector is exemplified by the Neighborhood Housing Services Program of the Federal Home Loan Bank Board, the Housing Reinvestment Task Force, and the Department of Housing and Urban Development. The program brings all the parties involved together in a common partnership:

-the neighborhood residents who want to improve the area;
-the local government willing to provide needed public services and improvements;
-a group of financial institutions that agree to reinvest in the neighborhood by making market-rate loans available to qualified individuals or making tax-deductible contributions to the program to support its operating costs.

Such partnerships, locally based, but with the resources of government at every level at their disposal, offer a promising model for helping to facilitate rediscovery of the sense of community in urban neighborhoods."[7]

• limited equity cooperatives as a means to increase the level of homeownership, especially among low income persons

• action at your state level to revise the financial fiscal base of your local government

Resources
Department of Housing and Urban Development
451 7th Street
Washington, D.C. 20410

National Association of Housing and Redevelopment Officials (NAHRO)
(6,800 individuals and 2,300 public agencies; focus: community rebuilding by community development, public housing, large-scale private or cooperative housing rehabilitation, and conservation of existing neighborhoods through code enforcement, voluntary citizen action, and government action; develops new techniques in administrative practice, financing, design, construction, management and community relations; aids in drafting legislation; consults with federal government agencies and other policy-making bodies; sponsors

workshops and seminars on housing and community development; maintains large library)
2600 Virginia Avenue, N.W.
Washington, D.C. 20037

National Association of Minority Contractors
1835 K Street, N.W.
Washington, D.C. 20006

National Center for Housing Management
(focus: housing management training)
1133 15th Street, N.W., Suite 611
Washington, D.C. 20005

National Leased Housing Association
(public and private individuals concerned/involved with the Section 8 Housing Assistance Program; informs members of Section 8 developments, represents members to HUD and Congress, holds training and educational seminars)
1800 M Street, N.W., Suite 400S
Washington, D.C. 20036

National Low Income Housing Coalition
(focus: improving and expanding low income housing programs)
215 Eighth Street, N.E.
Washington, D.C. 20002

National People's Action
(founded by Gail Cincotta; focus: pro neighborhood development and anti red-lining)
1123 W. Washington Blvd.
Chicago, IL 60607

National Rural Housing Coalition
(focus: improved government and private programs for rural housing; develops informational and educational materials)
1346 Connecticut Avenue, N.W.
Washington, D.C. 20036

FACTSHEET: Hunger

- hunger is a function of poverty

- the majority of hungry U.S. citizens are white although a greater percentage of the black population is hungry

- Native Americans suffer the most from malnutrition

- hunger in the U.S. is concentrated in the rural population, especially in the South and in Appalachia

- approximately 1 billion people suffer from chronic hunger and malnutrition (1 in 4 of the world's population)[1]

- the world's population is expected to double in another 35 years

- a child born today living an average life span will live in a world of 15 billion

- his grandchild will live on a planet with 60 billion others[2]

- the highest birthrate is in Asia, Africa, and Latin America

- India adds a million persons a month to its population[3]

- to feed the world's population in the year 2000 we will need to increase food supply 2½ times[4]

- with 6% of the world's population Americans consume 40% of the world's goods (including food)

- the average U.S. citizen consumes approximately 1,850 pounds of grain (most of it in meat and dairy products) per year

- the average person in poorer countries consumes 400 pounds of grain per year[5]

To Think About

- can we grow food fast enough to feed the world's growing population?

- "Every day the equivalent of twenty divisions of Martians invade this planet without their field rations."[6]

- "For just *one month's* average cost of the Vietnam war—$3.5 billion—the country could also have trained 100,000 agronomists or endowed four new Rockefeller Foundations for the fight against hunger overseas."[7]

- it has been estimated that just 10% of the total world armament budget could end malnutrition world-wide[8]

- are our country's present agricultural policies aimed at feeding people or making profits?

- can we solve or ameliorate the hunger problem in the world unless Americans change their eating and consuming habits?

- can we solve the hunger problem without confronting the poverty problem?

- Bill Moyers has said that "a global as opposed to regional approach to food, energy, capital, and development" is essential to resolving the hunger crisis.[9]

Resources

Agribusiness Council
345 E. 46th Street
New York, New York 10017

Bread for the World
6411 Chillum Place N.W.
Washington, D.C. 20012

The Children's Foundation
(focus: federal food assistance programs
for needy children and their families)
1420 New York Avenue, N.W., Suite 800
Washington, D.C. 20005

Conquest of Hunger Program or "the green revolution"
—one of five international programs of—
The Rockefeller Foundation
1133 Avenue of the Americas
New York, New York 10036

Department of Agriculture
14th and Independence Avenue, S.W.
Washington, D.C. 20250

Gamaliel
1335 N Street, N.W.
Washington, D.C. 20005

Institute for Food and Development Policy
2588 Mission Street
San Francisco, California 94110

Interreligious Taskforce on U.S. Food Policy
110 Maryland Avenue, N.E.
Washington, D.C. 20002

Meals for Millions/Freedom from Hunger Foundation,
Self-Help for a Hungry World
1800 Olympic Blvd., P.O. Drawer 680
Santa Monica, California 90406

Oxfam America
(international development agency which funds self-help programs in
Asia, Africa, and Latin America; focus: food and economic self-reliance)
115 Broadway
Boston, Massachusetts 02116

"Feeding All the Extra Billions: Endless Ingenuity Is Needed," Isaac Asimov, *Science Digest*, April 1979, pp. 15-19.

FACTSHEET: Legal Aid

- approximately 25,000,000 Americans are *very* poor (earning *less than $7,410* for a non-farm family of *four*) and presumably are unable to afford legal representation[1]

- there are approximately 850 legal services and defender programs in the U.S. for those unable to afford an attorney[2]

- the Legal Services Corporation (LSC) (established by the U.S. Congress in 1974) distributes federal funds to organizations across the country to provide legal services free to the poor (and is the backbone of 323 locally controlled programs operating out of 1,450 offices)

- with the help of LSC funds, in 1980 6,200 lawyers handled 1.5 million cases involving low income persons
    - –30.3% were domestic relations cases
    - –17.6% were housing related
    - –17.2% were related to income maintenance (food stamps, social security, etc.)
    - –13.7% were related to consumer finance disputes
    - –less than 1% of the LSC program cases have been "class action" cases[3]

- the LSC defines "poor" as under $10,000 in annual income for a family of four

- the Legal Services Corporation's budget is $321 million per year or approximately $10 per poor person (less than 3% of the LSC's budget goes to administrative costs; the remainder goes directly to servicing clients)

- President Reagan's budget called for eliminating the LSC and lumping legal assistance into a block grant to the states with the states not required to provide legal assistance[4]

- at this writing the U.S. House Judiciary Committee voted to reauthorize the LSC for 2 years reducing the funding from $321 million to $241 million per year[5]

- local bar associations administer an ABA program called the Lawyer Referral Service (LRS) for those who can afford to pay a very modest fixed fee for an initial consultation (so that a client can get an idea of the costs of legal work)[6]

To Think About

- "The right to a lawyer is not a basic right of citizens." (David Stockman)

- "There can be no equal justice where the kind of trial a man gets depends on the amount of money he has." (Griffin v. Illinois, U.S. Supreme Court)

- "Charity is no substitute for Justice withheld." (St. Augustine)

- "While the Reagan administration has proposed a tax cut for legal assistance to poor people, it did not propose a cut in the tax expenditure that allows businesses to deduct legal fees. The Library of Congress has found that this tax deduction costs the government $4 *billion* a year in lost revenues. . . ."[7]

Resources

Lawyer Referral Service, Standing Committee On
American Bar Association
1155 East 60th Street
Chicago, IL 60637

Legal Services Corporation
733 Fifteenth Street, N.W.
Washington, D.C. 20005

Legal Services Corporation
National Clearinghouse for Legal Services
(library service and publishes monthly review)
500 N. Michigan Avenue, Suite 1940
Chicago, IL 60611

National Legal Aid and Defender Association
1625 K Street, N.W.
Washington, D.C. 20006

Women's Legal Defense Fund
1424 16th Street, N.W.
Washington, D.C. 20036

FACTSHEET: Minorities

- 1980 Census population breakdown:[1]
  - 83.2% white (188,340,790)
  - 11.7% black (26,488,218)
  - 0.6% American Indian, Eskimos, Aleuts (1,418,195)
  - 1.5% Asian and Pacific Islander (3,500,636)
  - 3.0% other (6,756,986)

(above figures include 14,605,883 persons of Spanish origin—may be of any race)

- 53% of blacks live in the South

- during the 1970's immigration of blacks to the South appears to have been nearly equal to outmigration

- blacks comprise more than 1/5 of the population of 6 states (Mississippi, South Carolina, Georgia, Alabama, Maryland, North Carolina), and 70.3% of the population of the District of Columbia

- approximately 1/2 of 1.4 million American Indians, Eskimos and Aleuts live in the West making up 4-8% of the populations of New Mexico, South Dakota, Oklahoma, Arizona, and Montana

- nearly 60% of the 3.5 Asian and Pacific Islanders are located in the Pacific division, notably Hawaii (60.5% of the population of Hawaii, 5.3% of California's, less than 2% of every other state's population except Alaska's 2% and Washington's 2.5%)

- persons of Spanish origin comprise 6.4% of the population

- more than 60% of the 14.6 million persons of Spanish origin resided in 3 states in 1980: California, Texas, and New York

- persons of Spanish origin comprised more than 10% of the population of five states (New Mexico, Texas, California, Arizona, Colorado)[2]

- educational attainment of blacks
  - age 18-24, 42% of 3,500,000 have completed high school, 3.5% of 3,500,000 have completed college or more
  - age 25 & up, 30% of 12,227,000 have completed high school, 7.9% of 12,227,000 have completed college or more

- educational attainment of persons of Spanish origin
  - age 18-24: 38.4% of 1,699,000 have completed high school, 2.4% of 1,699,000 have completed college or more
  - age 25 & up: 25.6% of 5,367,000 have completed high school, 6.7% of 5,367,000 have completed college or more

- for comparison, educational attainment of whites
  - age 18-24: 46.9% of 23,984,000 have completed high school, 7.4% of 23,984,000 have completed college or more

-age 25 & up: 37.6% of 110,798,000 have completed high school, 17.2% of 110,798,000 have completed college or more[3]

- the general unemployment rate for all persons 16 years of age and older in May 1980, was 7.7%
  - 6.8% unemployment rate for whites (16 yrs. of age and older)
  - 13.6% for blacks and others (16 yrs. of age and older)
  - 14.6% for whites aged 16-19 years
  - 36.3% for blacks and others aged 16-19 years
  - 6.0% for white men aged 20 years and older
  - 12.6% for black and other men aged 20 years and older
  - 5.8% for white women aged 20 years and older
  - 10.9% for black and other women aged 20 years and older[4]

- 1978 median incomes
  - white males: $11,453 per year
  - black males: $ 6,861 per year
  - hispanic males: $ 8,380 per year
  - white females: $ 4,117 per year
  - black females: $ 3,707 per year
  - hispanic females: $ 3,788 per year[5]

- family incomes in 1978 dollars
  - white: $18,368 per year
  - black: $10,879 per year[6]

To Think About

- familiarity has not bred contempt—the results of a Louis Harris Poll for the National Conference of Christians and Jews:

	Percentage of whites who agreed	
	1967	1978
Blacks tend to have less ambition than whites	70	49
Blacks want to live off the handout	52	36
Blacks are more violent than whites	42	34
Blacks breed crime	32	29
Blacks have less native intelligence than whites	46	25
Blacks care less for the family than whites	34	18
Blacks are inferior to white people	29	15[7]

- "Perhaps someday in the future the term National Association for the Advancement of Colored People will metamorphose into the National Association for the Advancement of Civilized People and embrace us all."[8]

- social evil exists when social structures oppress human beings, violate human dignity, stifle freedom, impose gross inequality, when situations promote and facilitate individual acts of selfishness, when persons do not take responsibility for the evil being done[9]

Resources

A Better Chance
(aid for minority students—prepares student for college, conducts research and provides technical assistance on expanded educational opportunities for minority group students in secondary and higher education)
334 Boylston Street
Boston, Massachusetts 02116

American Indian Development Association
1145 Marine Drive
Bellingham, Washington 98225

American Indian Fund of the Association on
American Indian Affairs, Inc.
432 Park Avenue South
New York, New York 10016

Chicana Rights Project
(project of Mexican American Legal Defense & Education Fund, focus: Chicana women and employment, education and health)
517 Petroleum Commerce Bldg.
201 N. St. Mary's Street
San Antonio, Texas 78205

Chicano Training Center
(conducts seminars, institutes and workshops for institutions, agencies and organizations which extend services to the Chicano community)
3520 Montrose, Suite 216
Houston, Texas 77006

Commission on Civil Rights (U.S.)
1121 Vermont Avenue, N.W.
Washinton, D.C. 20425

Klanwatch
The Southern Poverty Law Center
1001 South Hull Street
Montgomery, Alabama 36101

Mexican American Legal Defense and Education Fund
28 Geary
San Franciso, California 94108

National Association for the Advancement of Colored People
1790 Broadway
New York, New York 10019

NAACP Legal Defense and Educational Fund
Ten Columbus Circle
New York, New York 10019

National Catholic Conference for Interracial Justice
1200 Varnum Street, N.E.
Washington, D.C. 20017

National Council of Negro Women
815 Second Avenue
New York, New York 10017

National Indian Youth Council, Inc.
201 Hermosa N.E.
Albuquerque, New Mexico 87108

National Urban League
500 E. 62nd Street
New York, New York 10021

United Negro College Fund
55 E. 52nd Street
New York, New York 10022

FACTSHEET: Welfare

(NOTE: At the time of this writing the funding levels and in some cases the future of certain welfare programs is undecided. In order to present the traditional scope of programs this factsheet will profile the welfare system at the close of the administration of President Carter.)

As of 1978, welfare programs included:

- Food Programs
  Child Nutrition Program
  Elderly Feeding Program
  Food Donations Program (Commodities)
  Food Stamp Program
  Special Supplemental Food Program for Women, Infants, and Children (WIC)
  Special Milk Program for Children

- Housing Programs
  Rural Housing Program
  Lower Income Housing Assistance Program (Section 8)
  Homeownership Assistance Program (Section 235)
  Rent Supplement Program
  Rental Housing Assistance Program (Section 236)
  Low-Rent Public Housing
  College Housing Grants

- Health Programs
  Public Health Services
  Medicaid
  Medicare (Social Security Hospital Insurance)
  Medicare (Social Security Supplementary Medical Insurance)
  Community Mental Health Program
  Community Drug Abuse Treatment Program
  Community Alcoholism Treatment Program

- Cash Assistance Programs
  Social Security Old Age and Survivors Insurance (OASI)
  Social Security Disability Insurance (DI)
  Special Benefits for Disabled Coal Miners
  Supplemental Security Income (SSI)
  Public Assistance Grants (AFDC)
  Refugee Assistance Programs
  General Assistance (General Relief)

- Employment and Work Training Programs
  Work Incentive Program (WIN)
  Comprehensive Employment and Training Assistance Program (CETA)
  Employment Service Program

    Job Corps
    Community Service Employment for Older Americans
    Unemployment Compensation Program
    Railroad Unemployment Compensation
    Workers Compensation Programs

- Education Programs
  Financial Assistance for Elementary and Secondary Education
  Financial Assistance for Higher Education

- Service and Miscellaneous Programs
  Public Assistance Services (AFDC)
  Human Development Services
  ACTION Domestic Programs
  Legal Services Program
  Veterans Benefit Programs
  Indian Benefit Programs
  Community Service Programs[1]

- fiscal 1978 saw over $190 billion spent on the top 12 income transfer and welfare programs

- approximately $153 billion spent on the 6 largest income transfer programs
  Social Security
  Medicare
  Unemployment Compensation
  Federal Civil Service Retirement
  Veterans Compensation Pensions
  Temporary Employment Assistance (creates public service jobs)

- in 1978 the 6 major welfare programs were
  Medicaid
  Aid to Families with Dependent Children (AFDC)
  Supplemental Security Income (SSI)
  Food Stamps
  Public Housing
  Child Nutrition[2]

- of the total of 44 welfare programs listed, 29 are financed completely from federal funds, 1 (General Assistance) is financed completely by state and local funds, 14 are shared programs (two types: AFDC, for example, provides either a federal match for state expenditures or a fixed federal percentage of the total expended; Unemployment Compensation, for example, includes a federal expenditure component unconnected to the amounts contributed by the state)[3]

- a strong correlation exists between the age of a program and how much it costs ("13 of the 'billion-dollar-plus' programs and 8 of the 10 most expensive programs were enacted prior to 1960")[4]

- in 1979 more than $250 billion was expended on welfare

- approximately 50 million Americans are beneficiaries of welfare programs

- approximately 5 million public and private workers distribute welfare payments and services[5]

To Think About

- "Radical welfare reform or any variety of a guaranteed income is politically impossible. No radical welfare reform plan can be devised that will simultaneously yield minimum levels of welfare benefits, financial incentives to work, and an overall cost to the taxpayers that are politically acceptable."[6]

- in welfare reform focus should be put on the strengths of the existing system and on "a deep appreciation for the attitudes of Americans toward caring for people who cannot care for themselves"[7]

- attitudinal changes toward welfare may be necessary and desirable (it might help to broaden the definition of welfare to include such direct cash transfers as income tax refunds for interest payments by homeowners, clearly a form of "welfare")

Resources

Department of Health and Human Services
200 Independence Avenue, S.W.
Washington, D.C. 20201

Department of Housing and Urban Development
451 7th Street, S.W.
Washington, D.C. 20410

Department of Education
Washington, D.C. 20202
(just to be sure, mark envelope "Please Forward If Necessary")

your state welfare offices
(usually at county seats and state capital)

FACTSHEET: Women

- there are 116,472,530 women in the U.S. (with a median age of 31.3)
- 96,671,164 are white
- 13,972,286 are black
- 717,188 are American Indian, Eskimo, Aleut
- 1,807,294 are Asian and Pacific Islander
- 3,304,598 are "other"
- of these, 7,327,624 are of Spanish origin (may be of any race)
- 15,241,532 women in the U.S. are age 65 and over[1]
- nearly 1 child in 5 in the U.S. lives with only 1 parent, 8 times out of 10 the mother[2]
- 35.6% of all female-headed families (3,300,000) were poor in 1978 (as opposed to 5.9% of all male-headed families)
- of all black female heads of households in 1978, 50.6% were poor (i.e., earning less than *$7,410* for a non-farm family of *4*)
- of all white female heads of households in 1978, 23.5% were poor[3]
- more than twice as many women held full-time jobs in 1979 (45% of all women) as did in 1969
- as of May 1979, 1/3 of those workers who hold second jobs are women[4]
- of 500 job categories in America, approximately 80% of women are in only 20 fields[5] (secretaries, sales clerks, waitresses, other low-paying entry level jobs)
- only 6% of women are managers[6]
- approximately 2% of all apprentices are women[7]
- only 17% of women belong to unions[8]
- 10% of state legislators are women
- 17 U.S. Congressmen (out of 535) are women[9]
- women still earn only about 59¢ for every dollar men earn, the same earnings gap as existed in *1939*
- women must work nearly 9 days to gross the same amount as men gross in 5 days (pay is especially low in textile plants and hospitals)
- women with 4 years of college still earn less than men with 8th grade educations

- 45% of married mothers with children under 6 work ouside the home (leaving 7 million children needing care with only 1.6 million licensed day-care openings)[10]

- homemakers need unemployment compensation, disability insurance, pension plans and all the normal fringe benefits of employment

- deadline for ratificiation of the Equal Rights Amendment is 1982

To Think About
- "Equality of rights under the law shall not be denied or abridged by the United States or by any State on account of sex."

Resources
Chicana Rights Project (Project of the Mexican American Legal Defense and Education Fund;
focus: Chicana women and employment, education and health)
517 Petroleum Commerce Building
201 N. St. Mary's Street
San Antonio, Texas 78205

Commission on Civil Rights (U.S.)
1121 Vermont Avenue, N.W.
Washington, D.C. 20425

Equal Employment Opportunity Commission (U.S.)
2401 E Street, N.W.
Washington, D.C. 20506

ERAmerica
1525 M Street, N.W.
Washington, D.C. 20005

National Council of Negro Women
815 Second Avenue
New York, New York 10017

National Organization for Women
425 13th Street, N.W., Suite 1048
Washington, D.C. 20004

National Women's Political Caucus
(focus: ERA; has lobbied for a bill to set up a national program
of day care)
1411 K. Street, N.W., Suite 1110
Washington, D.C. 20005

Women's Legal Defense Fund
1425 16th Street, N.W.
Washington, D.C. 20036

Your local conduit of Federal Legal Services Corporation funds may well have a Women's Law Project and in any case can assist low income women to gain legal representation

IV. Supplementary Address List

American Civil Liberties Union, 132 West 43rd Street, New York, NY 10036

ACORN (Association of Community Organizations for Reform Now) 628 Baronne Street, New Orleans, LA 70113, 504-523-1691

American Friends Service Committee, (focus: feeding, healing and sheltering victims of war and disaster), 1501 Cherry Street, Philadelphia, PA 19102, 215-241-7000

Americans for Common Sense (founder: George McGovern), 1825 Connecticut Avenue, N.W., Suite 214, Washington, D.C. 20009

Americans for Democratic Action, 1411 K Street, N.W., Washington, D.C. 20005

American National Red Cross, 17th & D Sts., N.W., Washington, D.C. 20006

Amnesty International—USA, 304 W. 58th Street, New York, NY 10023

Boys' Clubs of America, 771 First Avenue, New York, NY 10017

Campaign for Human Development, U.S. Catholic Conference, 1312 Massachusetts Avenue, N.W., Washington, D.C. 20005

Catholic Charities, National Conference of, 1346 Connecticut Avenue, N.W., Washington, D.C. 20036

Catholic Church Extension Society of the USA, 35 E.Wacker Drive, Chicago, IL 60601

Catholic Committee on Urban Ministry (CCUM), P.O. Box 544, Notre Dame, IN 46556

Catholic Peace Fellowship, 339 Lafayette Street, New York, NY 10012

Catholic Relief Services, 1011 First Avenue, New York, NY 10022

Catholics for Christian Political Action, 1609 K Street, N.W., Washington, D.C. 20006

Center for Science in the Public Interest, Nutrition Action Program, 1755 S Street, N.W., Washington, D.C. 20009

Citizen Labor/Energy Coalition, 600 W. Fullerton Parkway, Chicago, IL 60614

Committee for the Future of America (founder: Walter Mondale), P.O. Box 57433, Washington, D.C. 20037

Common Cause, 2030 M Street, N.W., Washington, D.C. 20036

Community Training and Development, 41 S. Main Street, Fond du Lac, WI 54935, 414-921-0225

Congress:
The Honorable_____
United States Senate
Washington, D.C. 20510

The Honorable_____
United States House of Representatives
Washington, D.C. 20510

(to call your senators or representatives, dial 202-224-3121 and ask for the member by name)

Democratic Party, National Headquarters, 1625 Massachusetts Avenue, N.W., Washington, D.C. 20036

Department of Commerce, 14th Street between Constitution Avenue and E Street, N.W., Washington, D.C. 20230

Department of Defense, The Pentagon, Washington, D.C. 20301

Department of Domestic Social Development, U.S. Catholic Conference, 1312 Massachusetts Avenue, N.W., Washington, D.C. 20005

Department of Justice, Constitution Avenue and 10th Street, N.W., Washington, D.C. 20530

Department of State, 2201 C Street, N.W., Washington, D.C. 20520

Department of Transportation, 400 7th Street, S.W., Washington, D.C. 20590

Department of the Treasury, 1500 Pennsylvania Avenue, N.W., Washington, D.C. 20220

Federal Communications Commission, 1919 M Street, N.W., Washington, D.C. 20554

Federal Trade Commission, Pennsylvania Avenue at Sixth Street, N.W., Washington, D.C. 20580

Food and Drug Administration, 5600 Fishers Lane, Rockville, MD 20857, 301-443-3170

Foundations: (for a *total overview* of Foundations, check your library for *The Foundation Directory*, The Foundation Center: New York, 1979 or after)

• *The Ford Foundation*, 320 East 43rd Street, New York, NY 10017, 212-573-5000

• *The Mott (Charles Stewart) Foundation*, Mott Foundation Building, Flint, Michigan 48502, 313-238-5651

• *The Rockefeller Foundation*, 1133 Avenue of the Americas, New York, NY 10036, 212-869-8500

Institute for (the Education to) Peace and Justice, 2747 Rutger, St. Louis, MO 63104

Institute for Social Justice, 628 Baronne Street, New Orleans, LA 70113

Joint Action in Community Service (a non-profit national volunteer organization whose major responsibilities are to the Department of Labor Job Corps Program), 1730 Rhode Island Avenue, N.W., Washington, D.C. 20036, 202-223-0912

League of Woman Voters
1730 M Street
Washington, D.C. 20036

Lutheran World Relief, 360 Park Avenue South, New York, NY 10010

National Association of Broadcasters (NAB), 1771 N Street, N.W., Washington, D.C. 20036

National Association of Manufacturers, 1776 F Street, N.W., Washington, D.C. 20006, 202-331-3700

National Association of Mental Health, 1800 N. Kent Street, Arlington, VA 22209

National Association of Neighborhoods, 1651 Fuller Street, N.W., Washington, D.C. 20009, 202-332-7766

National Center for Community Action, 1328 New York Avenue, N.W., Washington, D.C. 20005, 202-667-8970

National Center for Urban Ethnic Affairs, 1521 16th Street, N.W., Washington, D.C. 20036

National Community Development Association (focus: those dealing with Community Development funds), 1620 Eye Street, N.W., Suite 503, Washington, D.C. 20006, 202-293-7587

National Endowment for the Arts, 2401 E Street, N.W., Washington, D.C. 20506

National Farm Worker Ministry, 1430 W. Olympic Blvd., Los Angeles, CA 90015

National Governors' Association, Hall of the States, 444 N. Capitol, Washington, D.C. 20001, 202-624-5300

National League of Cities (a federation of state leagues and municipalities representing 900 municipalities plus individual cities; focus: develops and puts in effect National Municipal Policy, a statement of major municipal goals in the U.S.; represents municipalities with Congress and federal agencies; maintains large library, plus information and consultation service; publishes *Nation's Cities* Weekly), 1301 Pennsylvania Avenue, N.W., Washington, D.C. 20004

National Peace Academy Campaign (focus: establishment of a U.S. Academy for Peace and Conflict Resolution), 1625 Eye Street, N.W., Suite 726, Washington, D.C. 20006

National Training and Information Center (NTIC), 115 West Washington Street, Chicago, IL 60607

Opportunities Industrialization Centers of America, 100 W. Coulter Street, Philadelphia, PA 19144, 215-849-3010

Progressive Alliance (alliance of civil rights, social, civic, consumer, and labor organizations), 1625 L Street, N.W., Washington, D.C. 20036, 202-452-4800

(Ralph Nader) Center for Study of Responsive Law, P.O. Box 19367, Washington, D.C. 20036

Republican Party, National Headquarters, 310 First Street, S.E., Washington, D.C. 20003

Television Networks

- *American Broadcasting Company* (ABC), 1330 Avenue of the Americas, New York, NY 10019

- *Canadian Broadcasting Corporation* (CBC), 1500 Bronson Avenue, Ottawa, Ontario, Canada K1G3J5

- *Columbia Broadcasting System* (CBS), 51 W. 52nd Street, New York, NY 10019

- *Metromedia*, 485 Lexington Avenue, New York, NY 10017

- *National Broadcasting Company* (NBC), 30 Rockefeller Plaza, New York, NY 10020

- *Public Broadcasting Service* (PBS), 609 Fifth Avenue, New York, NY 10017

- *Westinghouse Broadcasting* (Group W), 90 Park Avenue, New York, NY 10016

United Farm Workers of America, LaPaz, Keene, CA 93531

U.S. Conference of Mayors, 1620 Eye Street, N.W., Washington, D.C. 20006

U.S. Government Printing Office, Washington, D.C. 20402

The White House, 1600 Pennsylvania Avenue, Washington, D.C. 20500

The World Council of Churches, U.S. Conference for, 475 Riverside Drive, New York, NY 10027

Local Address List (fill this in yourself)

Notes

Theoretical Orientations/Ethical Considerations

1. Peter L. Berger, *Pyramids Sacrifice: Political Ethics and Social Change*, Anchor Press-Doubleday: New York, 1976, p. 183.

2. Louis J. Halle, *Out of Chaos*, Houghton Mifflin Company: Boston, 1977, p. 603.

3. Johannes B. Metz, *Theology of the World*, Seabury Press, New York, 1973, p. 107.

4. Berger, *Pyramids of Sacrifice*, p. 183.

5. Peter L. Berger and Richard J. Neuhaus, *To Empower People: The Role of Mediating Structures in Public Policy*, American Enterprise Institute for Public Policy Research: Washington, D.C., 1977, p. 40.

6. Berger, *Pyramids of Sacrifice*, p. 249.

7. Ibid.

8. George McGovern, from a lecture given at Northwestern University, March 30, 1981, reprinted in "Common Sense on the Issues," Americans for Common Sense, 1825 Connecticut Avenue, N.W., Suite 214, Washington, D.C. 20009.

9. Carlos Castaneda, *Tales of Power*, Pocket Books—Simon and Schuster: New York, 1974, p. 55.

10. Berger, *Pyramids of Sacrifice*, pp. 246, 247.

11. *The Encyclopedia of Philosophy*, Paul Edwards (ed.), Macmillan: New York, 1967, Volume 7, p. 282.

12. Berger, *Pyramids of Sacrifice*, p. 252.

The Aged

1. 1980 U.S. Census figures.

2. (facts 4-8) G. Dyer, "Our Graying World," *World Press Review*, December, 1979, p. 31.

3. Margie Casady, "Senior Syndromes," *Human Behavior*, March 1976, p. 46.

4. Crowley and Cloud, "Aging Advocacy at the National Level," *Aging*, July/August 1979, p. 13.

5. Sylvia Porter, "Retirement Plan Saves Taxes," *The Oklahoma Journal*, April 22, 1976, p. 9.

6. (facts 15-19) Deak and Smith, "Inflation and the Elderly," *Aging*, September/October 1979, pp. 4, 5.

7. Dyer, "Our Graying World," p. 32.

8. Deak and Smith, "Inflation and the Elderly," p. 5.

9. J.K. Eckert, "The Unseen Community: Understanding the Older Hotel Dweller," *Aging*, January/February 1979.

10. R. Benedict, "Making the Health Care System Responsive to the Needs of the Elderly," *Aging*, May/June 1979, p. 26.

11. (facts 24 and 25) Jack Anderson, "What Congress Is Failing To Do for You," *50-Plus*, January 1980, pp. 37, 38.

12. P.K. Snyder and A. Way, "Alcoholism and the Elderly," *Aging*, January/February 1979, p. 8.

Child Development and Youth

1. "Parade," *Chicago Sun-Times*, August 30, 1981, p. 19.

2. (facts 2-6) 1980 U.S. Census figures, Department of Commerce.

3. (facts 7 and 8) S. Copans, H. Krell, J.H. Gundy, J. Rogan, F. Field, "Stresses of Treating Child Abuse Children-at-Risk Program," *Children Today*, January/February 1979, p. 22.

4. (facts 9 and 10) "Fatal Blunder," *Newsweek*, March 5, 1979, p. 94.

5. Ibid., p. 96.

6. (facts 12 and 13) Ibid., p. 94.

7. (facts 14-16) Ibid., p. 96.

8. *The World Almanac and Book of Facts*, Newspaper Enterprise Association, Inc.: New York, 1981, p. 177.

9. "Fatal Blunder," *Newsweek*, p. 98.

Criminal Justice

1. (facts 4-7) "Justice Assistance News" (citing FBI Crime Index), U.S. Department of Justice, May 1981, p. 1. (All crimes include attempts.)

2. "The Plague of Violent Crime," *Newsweek*, March 23, 1981, p. 50.

3. (facts 8 and 9) FBI Crime Index.

4. "The Plague of Violent Crime," p. 48.

5. *Chicago Tribune*, Friday, December 12, 1980, Section 3, p. 2.

6. FBI Crime Index.

7. (facts 13 and 14) *Chicago Tribune*, December 12, 1980, Section 3, p. 4.

8. Figures from a *National Law Journal* Survey

9. J.Q. Wilson, *Thinking About Crime*, Basic Books, Inc.: New York, 1975, p. 186.

10. (facts 19 and 20) "The Plague of Violent Crime," p. 53.

11. (facts 21 and 22) "Criminal Justice Newsletter," National Council on Crime and Delinquency, May 11, 1981, pp. 6, 7.

12. "National Prison Project Status Report: The Courts and Prisons," ACLU, February 1, 1981, p. 1.

13. (facts 24 and 25) "The Plague of Violent Crime," p. 54.

14. L. Radzinowicz and J. King, *The Growth of Crime: The International Experience*, Basic Books, Inc.: New York, 1977, p. 292.

15. "The Plague of Violent Crime," p. 54.

16. (facts 28-30) "Justice Assistance News," U.S. Department of Justice, March 1981, p. 6 (from statistics appearing in "Parole in the United States: 1979," Bureau of Justice Statistics, Washington, D.C. 20531).

17. "Criminal Justice Newsletter," National Council on Crime and Delinquency, September 29, 1980, p. 5.

18. For the "Criminal Court Monitoring Handbook," write the Fund for Modern Courts, 36 West 44th Street, Room 711, New York, New York 10036 (include $1.00).

19. Wilson quoting Arnold Barnett, Daniel J. Kleitman, and Richard C. Larson, "On Urban Homicide," working paper, WP-04-74, Operations Research Center, MIT, March 1974.

20. Cf. N. Morris, "The Law Is a Busybody: Crimes Without Victims," *New York Times Magazine*, April 1, 1973.

Drugs and Addiction

1. Committee on Alcoholism and Drug Abuse for Greater New Orleans, Inc., *First Aid Manual for Drug Abuse Emergencies and Community Resources Directory*, p. 4.

2. Morrow and Suzanne Wilson (eds.), *Drugs in American Life*, H.W. Wilson Co.: New York, 1975, p. 87.

3. (facts 6-8) Ibid., p. 106.

4. A. and V. Silverstein, *Alcoholism*, J.B. Lippicott Co.: Philadelphia and New York, 1975, p. 72.

5. D.R. Wesson and D.E. Smith, *Barbiturates: Their Use, Misuse and Abuse*, Human Sciences Press: New York, 1977, p. 13.

6. D. Dusek and D.A. Girdano, *Drugs: A Factual Account*, Addison-Wesley Publishing Co.: Reading, Massachusetts, 1980, p. 126.

7. Ibid., pp. 230, 232, 233.

8. Ibid., p. 230.

9. Ibid., p. 233.

10. Ibid., p. 126.

Economic Development

1. (facts 1-6) *The World Almanac and Book of Facts*, Newspaper Enterprise Association, Inc.: New York, 1981, p. 133.

2. "The President's National Urban Policy Report, 1980, Executive Summary," U.S. Department of Housing and Urban Development, August 1980, p. 15.

3. "The President's National Urban Policy Report, 1978," Department of Housing and Urban Development, August 1978, p. 71.

4. (facts 8 and 9) "The President's National Urban Policy Report, 1980, Executive Summary," HUD, p. 15.

5. (facts 10 and 11) "Federal Activities in Urban Economic Development," prepared for the Economic Development Administration of the U.S. Dept. of Commerce by G. Vernez, R. J. Vaughan, R. K. Yin, A. H. Pascal, EDA, April 1979, p. 4.

6. Ibid., p. vii.

7. Ibid.

8. Ibid.

9. Ibid., p. viii.

10. Ibid., pp. xvi, xvii.

11. Ibid., p. xix.

12. Neal R. Peirce, "Social Investment Urged for Pension Funds," *Nation's Cities Weekly*, April 27, 1981, p. 4.

13. J. K. Galbraith, *The Nature of Mass Poverty*, Harvard University Press: Cambridge, Massachusetts, 1979, p. 108.

14. Ibid., p. 100.

Education

1. The World Almanac and Book of Facts, Newspaper Enterprise Association, Inc.: New York, 1981, p. 274.

2. Ibid., p. 266.

3. (facts 4 and 5) Ibid., p. 266.

4. Ibid., p. 269.

5. (facts 7-9) Ibid., p. 267.

6. Ibid., p. 265.

7. N. Postman and C. Weingartner, *Teaching as a Subversive Activity*, Dell Publishing Co., Inc.: New York, 1969, pp. 2,3.

8. Ibid., p. 154.

9. J. Gardner, *The Changing Classroom*, Carol Goodell (ed.), Ballantine Books: New York, 1973, p. 117.

10. Ibid., p. 117.

11. N. Postman and C. Weingartner, *Teaching as a Subversive Activity*, p. 81.

12. M. Adler, *Reforming Education*, Westview Press: Boulder, Colorado, 1977, p. 195.

13. M. Rafferty, *The Changing Classroom*, Carol Goodell (ed.), p. 91.

The Environment

1. Melvin A. Benarde, *Our Precarious Habitat*, W. W. Norton and Co.: New York, 1970, p. 172.

2. Ibid.

3. *American Planning Association News*, February 1979, p. 2.

4. "CBS Evening News with Dan Rather," October 15, 1981.

5. Thor Heyerdahl, "How To Kill an Ocean," *Saturday Review*, November 29, 1975, p. 18.

6. (facts 7 and 8) Ibid., p. 15.

7. (facts 9-11) "Are We Running Out of Water?" *Newsweek*, February 23, 1981, p. 26.

8. Ibid., p. 30.

9. (facts 13-15) Ibid., p. 27.

10. "Energy: A Special Report in the Public Interest," *National Geographic*, February 1981, p. 27.

11. Ibid., pp. 68, 69.

12. Ibid., p. 38.

13. Ibid., p. 64.

14. Ibid., p. 61.

15. Ibid., p. 63.

16. ibid., p. 59.

17. Ibid., p. 67.

18. Sheila Macmanus, *Charismatic Social Action*, Paulist Press: New York, 1977, p. 55.

19. Michael McCloskey, "The Time It Takes," Wilderness 1976 Sierra Club Engagement Calendar.

20. Jacques-Yves Cousteau, letter from The Cousteau Society, 1981.

21. J. Cousteau, "The Ocean, Survival, and the Pursuit of Happiness," *Saturday Review*, November 27, 1976, p. 55.

22. "What Next for Nuclear Power: Kemeny Report," *U.S. News and World Report*, November 12, 1979, p. 33.

The Handicapped

1. (facts 1-10) S. Kleinfield, *The Hidden Minority: America's Handicapped*, Little Brown: Boston and Toronto, 1979, p. 32.

2. (facts 11-13) "Jobs for Handicapped Persons: A New Era in Civil Rights," Public Affairs Committee pamphlet #557, New York, 1978, p. 3.

3. (facts 14-18) Figures from a Fortune 500 corporation study quoted in "Hire the Handicapped," Job Service Pamphlet, Illinois Department of Labor, Bureau of Employment Security.

4. (facts 19-21) "The Forgotten Warriors," *Time*, July 13, 1981, p. 20.

5. (facts 22 and 23) Ibid., p. 21.

6. (facts 24-26) "Jobs for Handicapped Persons: A New Era in Civil Rights," Public Affairs Committee, pp. 4, 6, 7.

7. T. M. Madison, "Those Who Speak Up," *MH* (Mental Hygiene) Spring 1975, p. 29.

Housing

1. Chester W. Hartman, *Housing and Social Policy*, Prentice-Hall, Inc.: Englewood Cliffs, New Jersey, 1975, pp. 8, 9.

2. "CBS Evening News with Dan Rather," October 19, 1981.

3. (facts 4 and 5) "The President's National Urban Policy Report, 1980: Executive Summary," Department of Housing and Urban Development, p. 18.

4. (facts 6-11) "Federal Housing Policy: Current Programs and Recurring Issues," Congress of the United States: Congressional Budget Office, June 1978, pp. v, xii-xv.

5. "The President's National Urban Policy Report, 1978," Department of Housing and Urban Development, p. 74.

6. (facts 13-16) "Developing a Local Housing Strategy, A Guidebook for Local Government," Department of Housing and Urban Development, November 1978, p. 15.

7. "The President's National Urban Policy Report, 1978," Department of Housing and Urban Development, p. 76.

Hunger

1. "A Survival Summit," *Newsweek*, October 26, 1981, p. 37.

2. (facts 6-8) J. Archer, *Hunger on Planet Earth*, Thomas Y. Crowell Company: New York, 1977, p. 25.

3. Ibid., p. 25.

4. Ibid., p. 165.

5. (facts 13 and 14) "An Alternate Diet," a pamphlet, Bread for the World: New York.

6. Archer (quoting British scientist Ritchie Calder), *Hunger on Planet Earth*, p. 25.

7. Ibid., pp. 193-94.

8. Ibid., p. 194 (quoting England's Lord Boyd Orr)

9. Ibid., p. 194.

Legal Aid

1. *The World Almanac and Book of Facts*, Newspaper Enterprise Association, Inc.: New York, 1981, p. 277.

2. J. L. Barkas, *The Help Book*, Charles Scribner's Sons: New York, 1979, p. 482.

3. (facts 3 and 4) Patricia Theiler, "The Case for Legal Services Corporation," *Common Cause*, June 1981, p. 35.

4. Ibid.

5. Robert McClory, "Legal Services Countdown—Fighting Off the Wolves," *Chicago Lawyer*, 1981, p. 3.

6. Barkas, *The Help Book*, p. 484.

Minorities

1. Counts by race and Spanish origin are provisional.

2. (facts 1-9) from U.S. Dept. of Commerce advance reports on the 1980 U.S. Census.

3. *The World Almanac and Book of Facts*, Newspaper Enterprise Association, Inc.: New York, 1981, p. 270.

4. Ibid., p. 177.

5. Ibid., p. 271.

6. Ibid., p. 269.

7. "A New Racial Poll," *Newsweek*, February 26, 1979, p. 48.

8. W. H. Moses, "After 78 Years," *Newsweek*, December 31, 1979, p. 15.

9. Campaign for Human Development—definition of "social sin."

Welfare

1. C. D. Hobbs, *The Welfare Industry*, The Heritage Foundation: Washington, D.C., 1978, pp. 3, 4.

2. (facts 8-10) M. Anderson, *Welfare: The Political Economy of Welfare Reform in the United States*, Hoover Institution of Stanford University: Palo Alto, California, 1978, pp. 27—30.

3. Hobbs, *The Welfare Industry*, p. 14.

4. Ibid., p. 18.

5. (facts 13-15) Ibid., p. 7.

6. Anderson, *Welfare: The Political Economy of Welfare Reform in the United States*, p. 133.

7. Ibid., pp. 153, 154.

Women

1. (facts 1-8) from U. S. Dept. of Commerce advance reports on the 1980 U. S. Census.

2. *The World Almanac and Book of Facts*, Newspaper Enterprise Association, Inc.: New York, 1981, p. 277.

3. (facts 10-12) Ibid., p. 133.

4. (facts 13 and 14) Ibid., p. 277.

5. E. C. Smeal, "Women's Concerns Will Become Really Major Issues," *U.S. News and World Report*, October 15, 1979, p. 79.

6. *The World Almanac and Book of Facts*, Newspaper Enterprise Association, Inc., p. 277.

7. Smeal, "Women's Concerns Will Become Really Major Issues," p. 79.

8. *The World Almanac and Book of Facts*, Newspaper Enterprise Association, Inc., p. 277.

9. (facts 19 and 20) Smeal, "Women's Concerns Will Become Really Major Issues," p. 79.

10. (facts 21-24) *The World Almanac and Book of Facts*, Newspaper Enterprise Association, Inc., p. 277.

"There is no comparison between that which is lost by not succeeding, and that which is lost by not trying."
—**Francis Bacon**

WITHDRAWN